ALL I WANT FOR CHRISTMAS

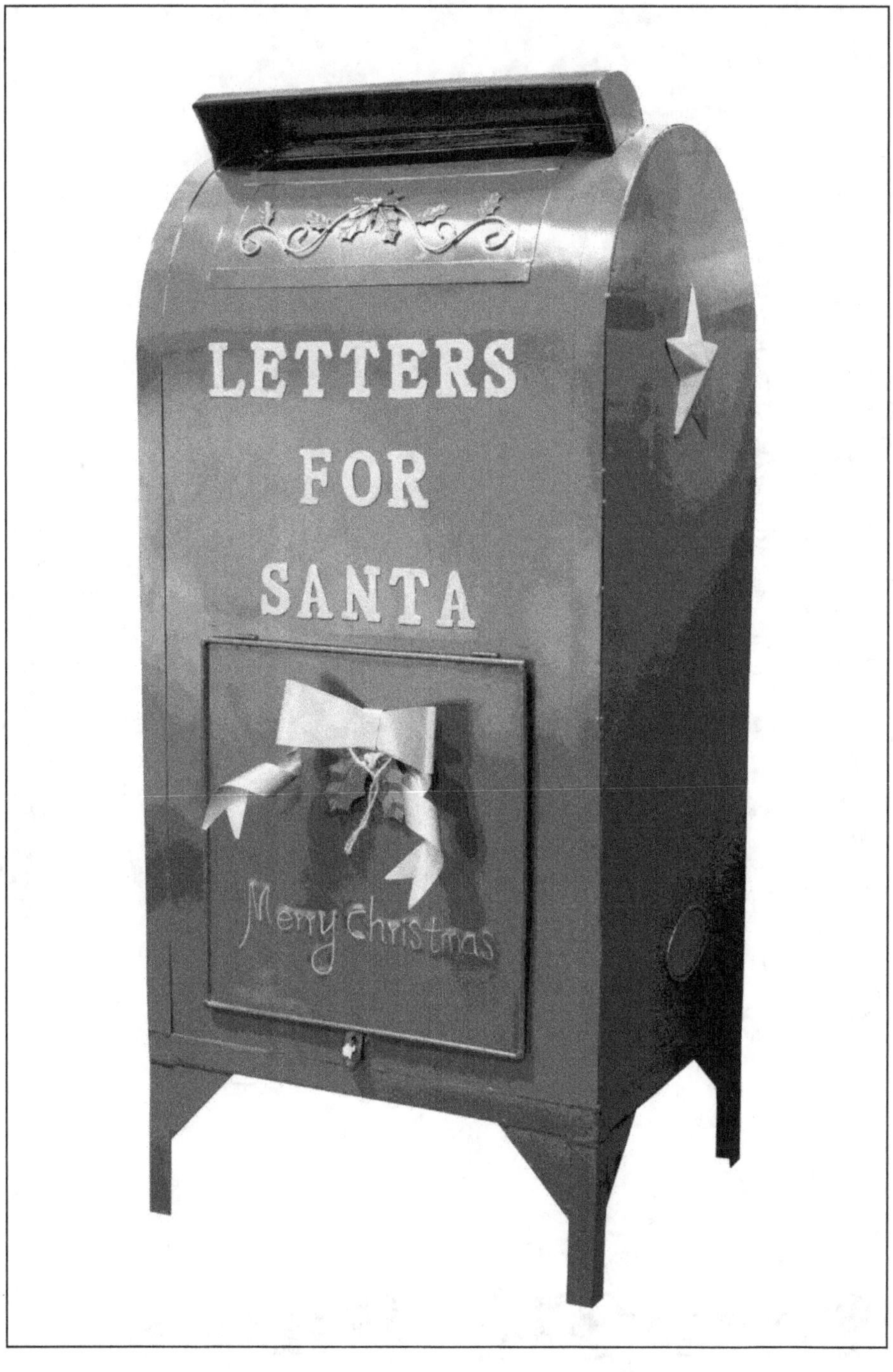

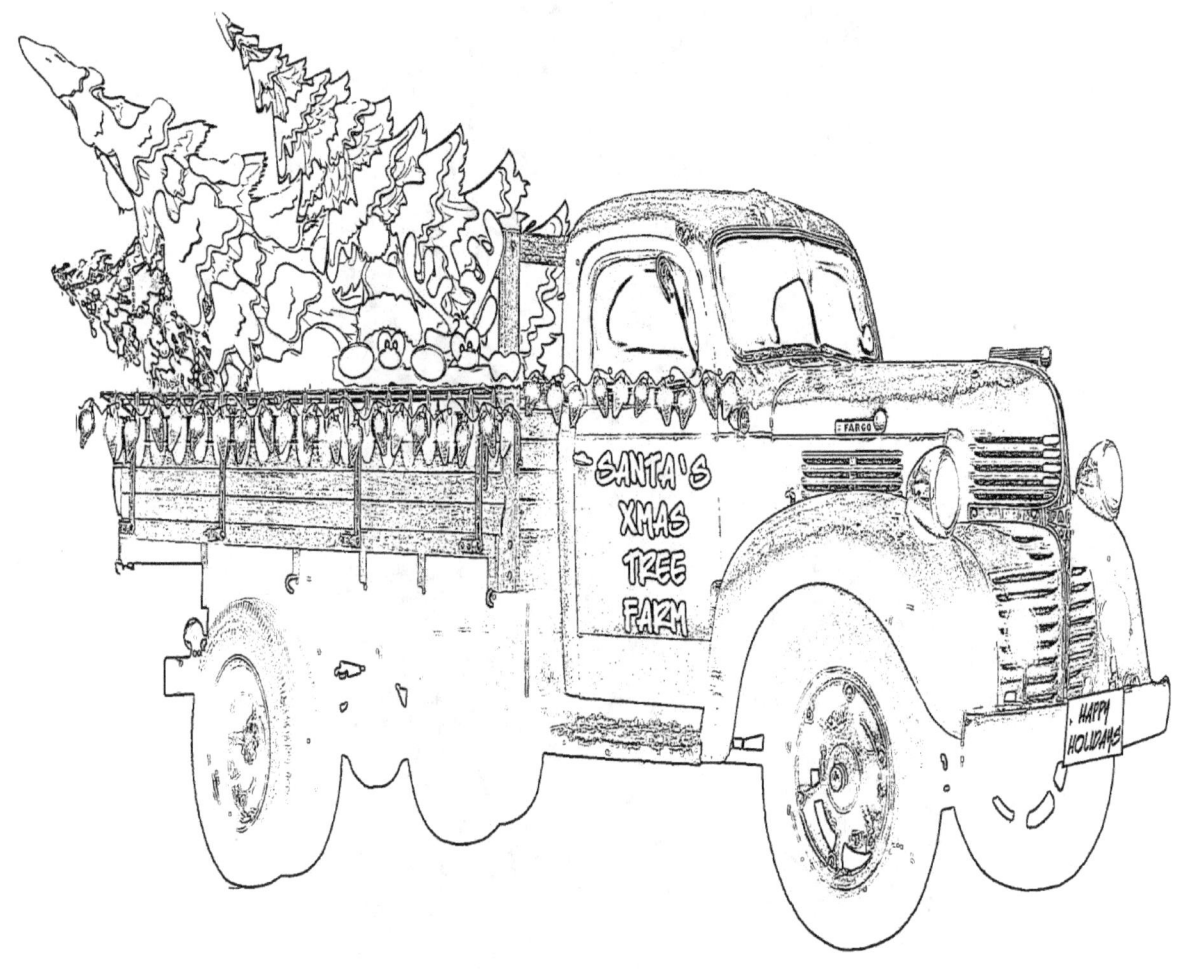

Sample Page

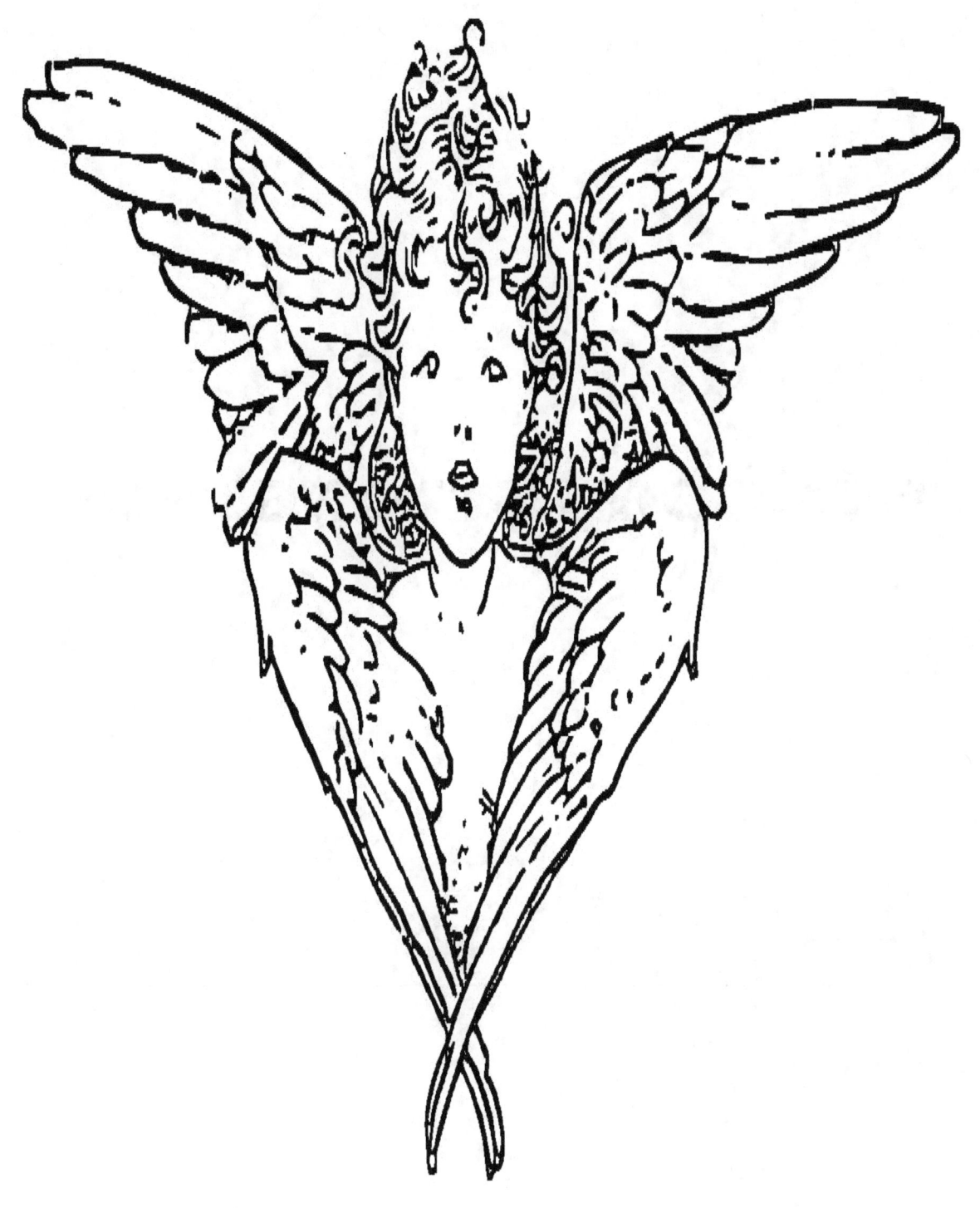

Sample Page

THIS BOOK BELONGS TO:

_____

Copyrighted Material

All rights reserved. This publication may not be reproduced or distributed. This includes mechanical or electronic methods. Photocopying or recording is prohibited. Prior written permission must be obtained from the publisher.

Introduction:

"All I WANT FOR CHRISTMAS, LETTERS FOR SANTA"

is a juvenial coloring book with some activity pages. It is intended for children ages 5 and up. It will stimulate their minds, as they engage in coloring some of their favorite images. Each page will help them to embrace the essence and true meaning of the Christmas holiday season.

My Wish List To Santa:

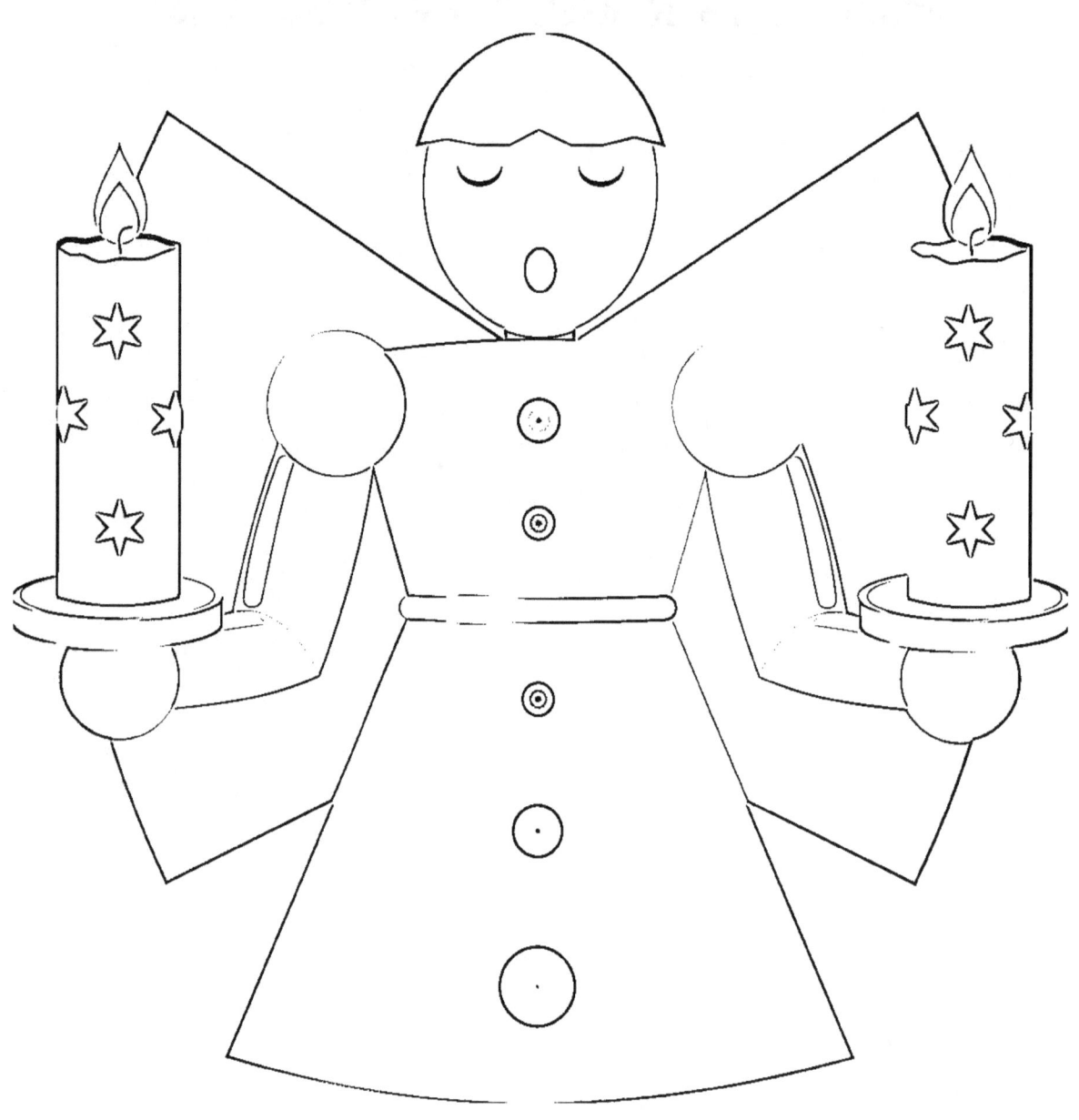

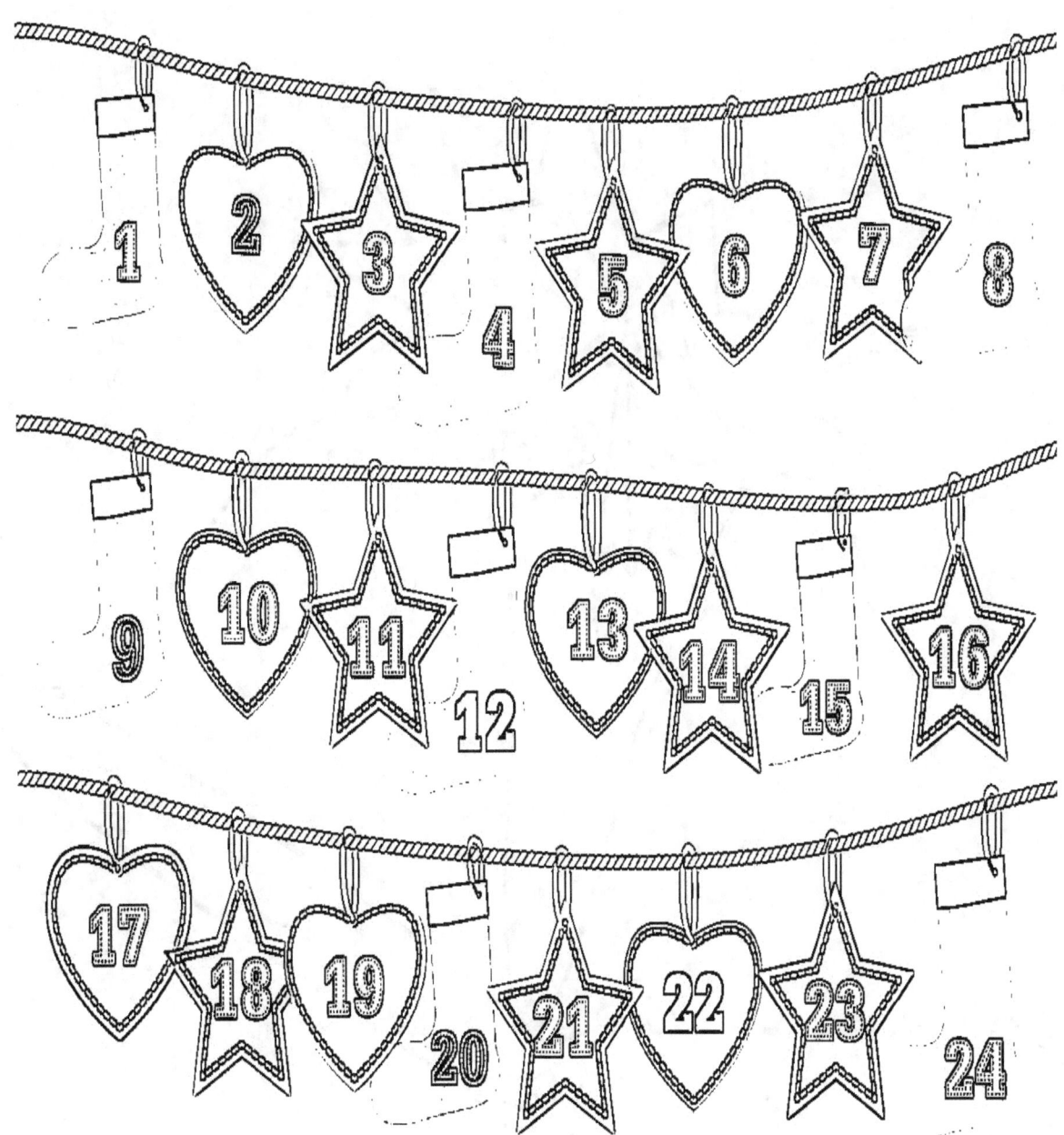

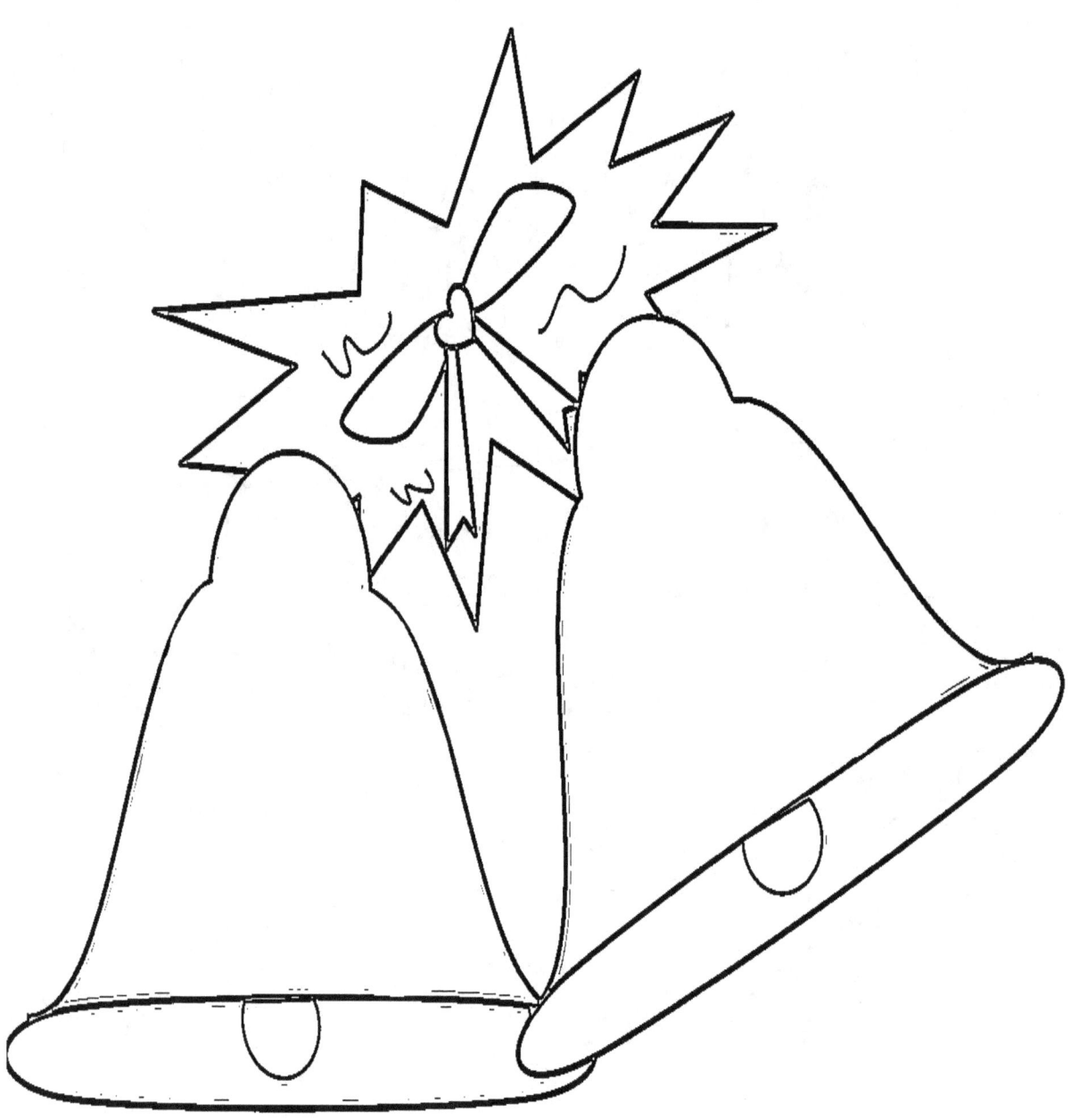

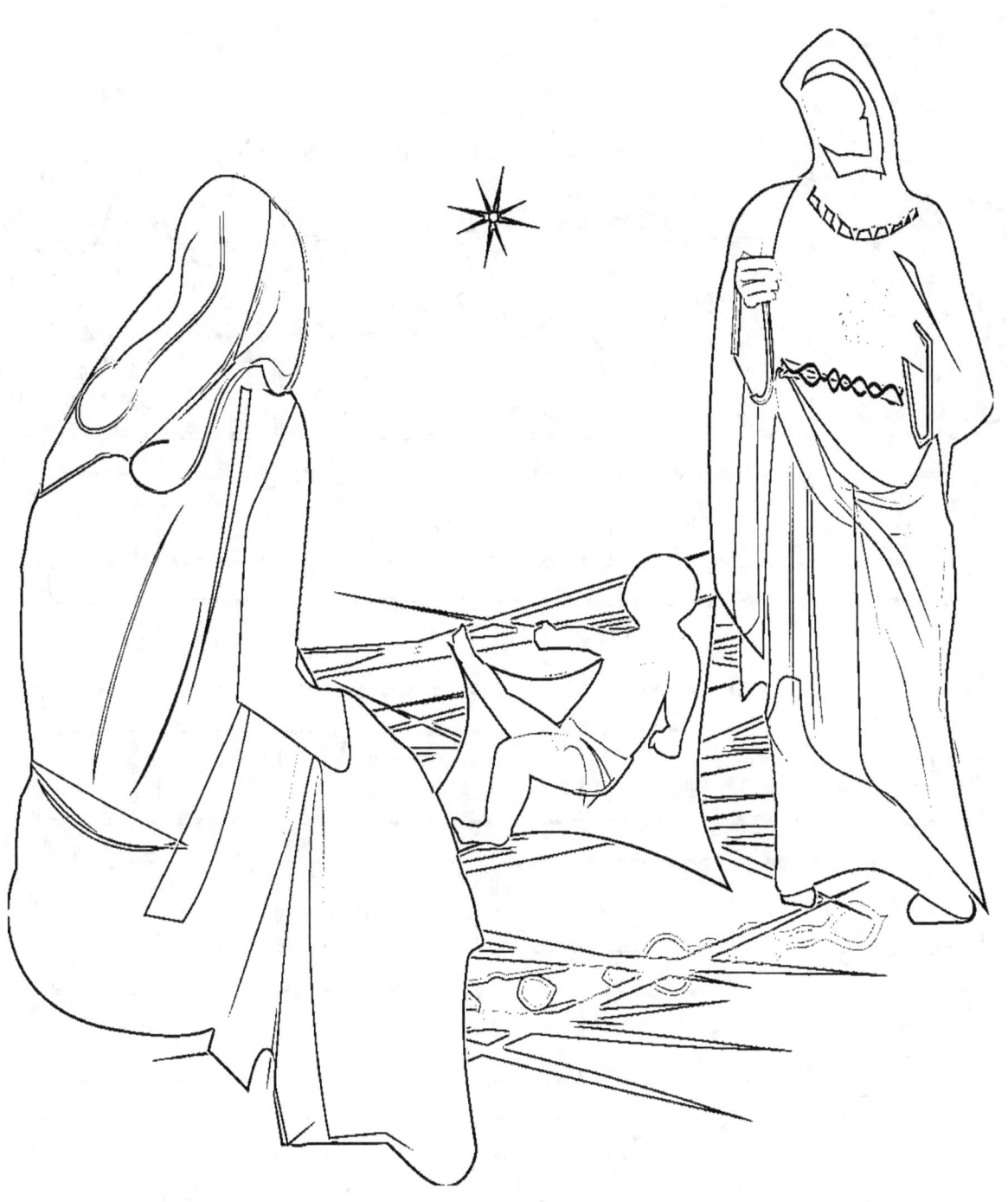

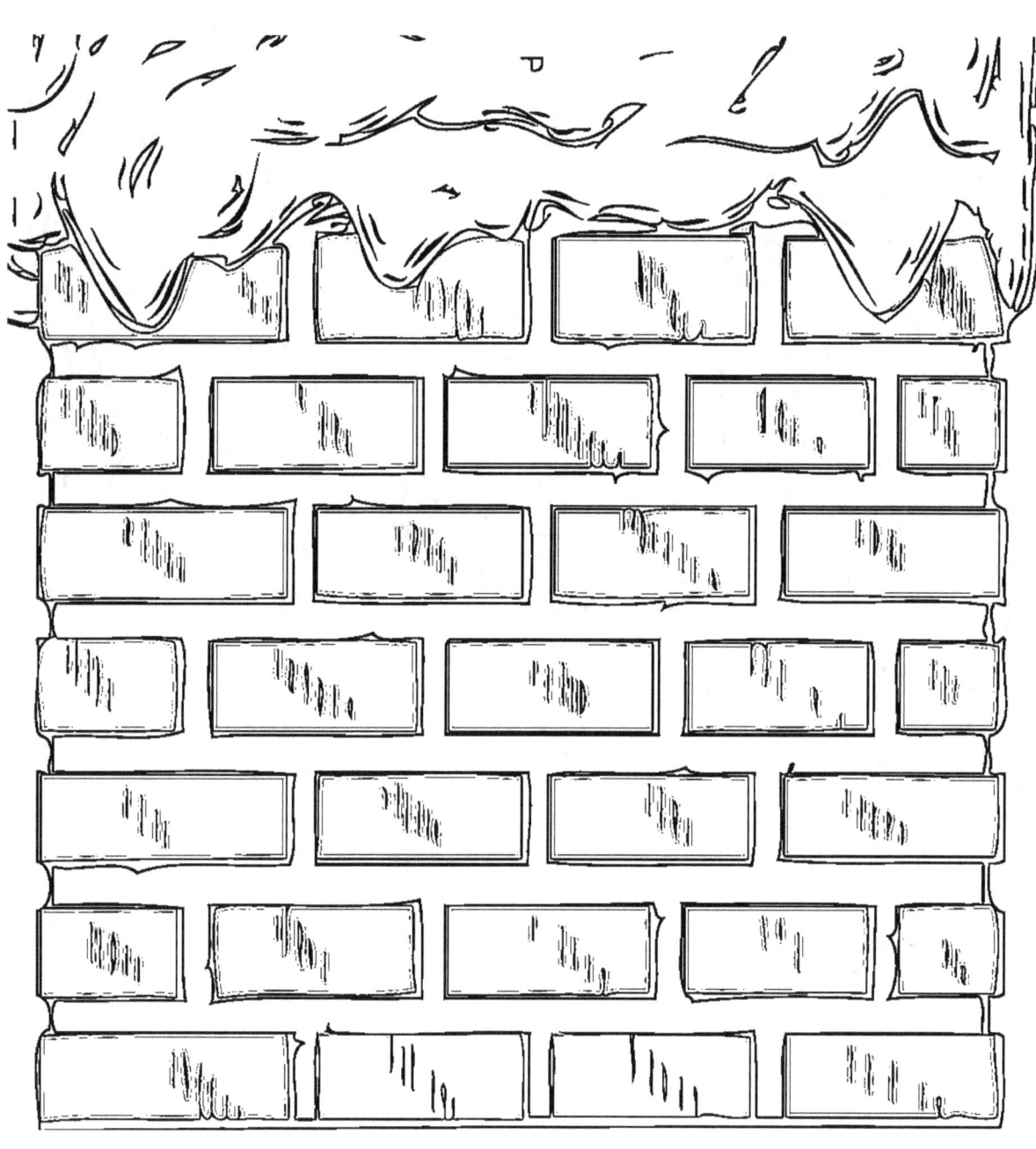

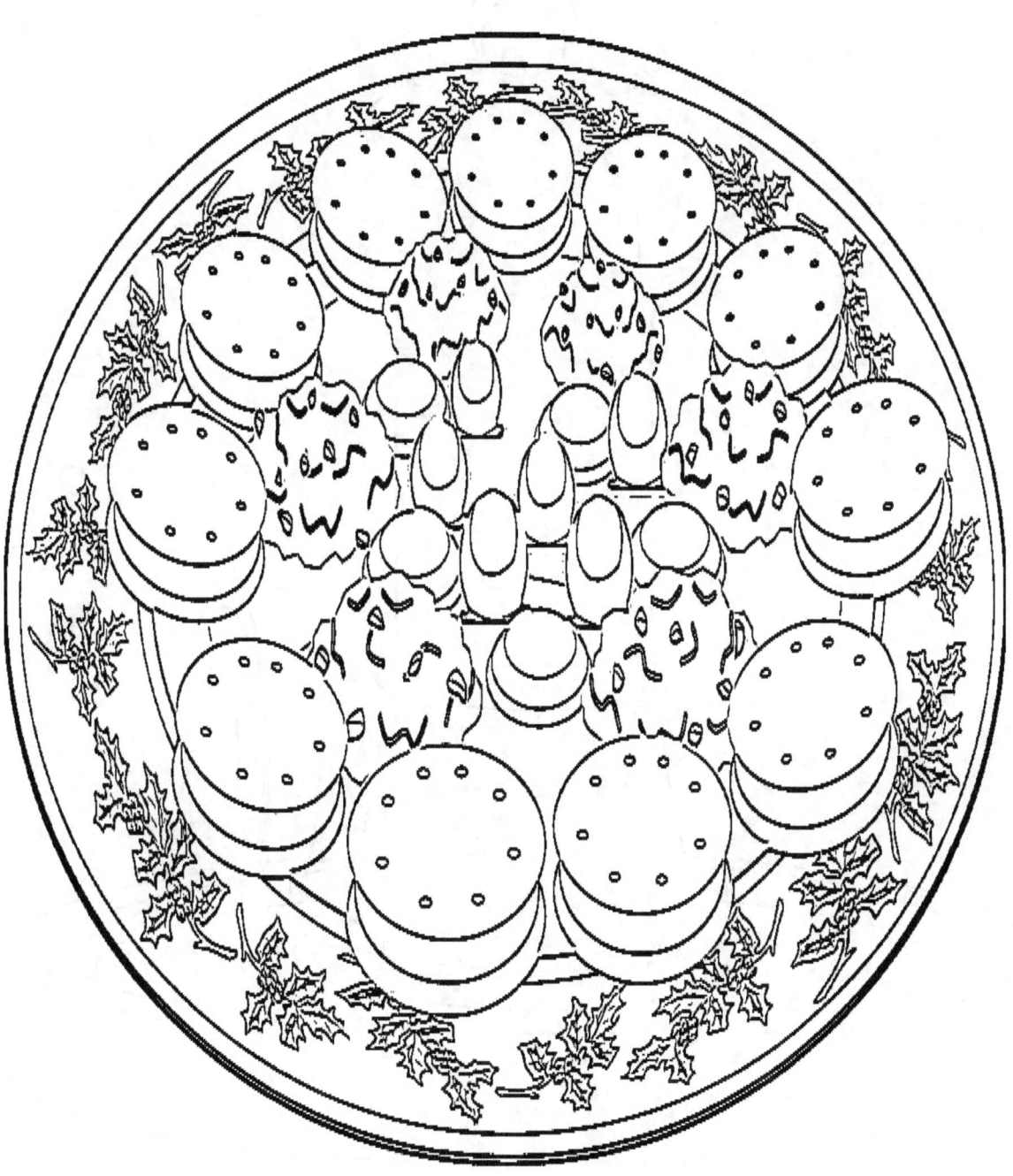

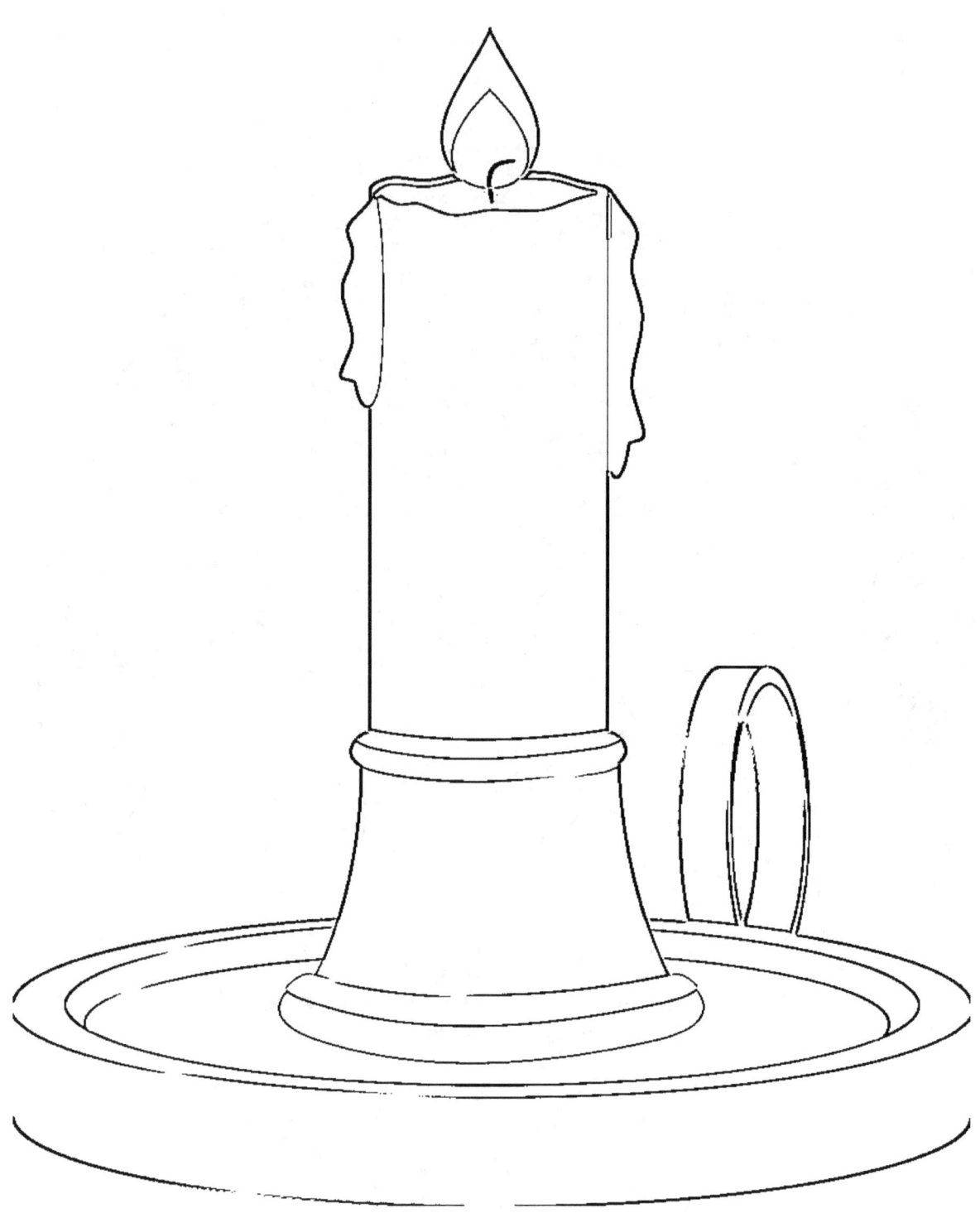

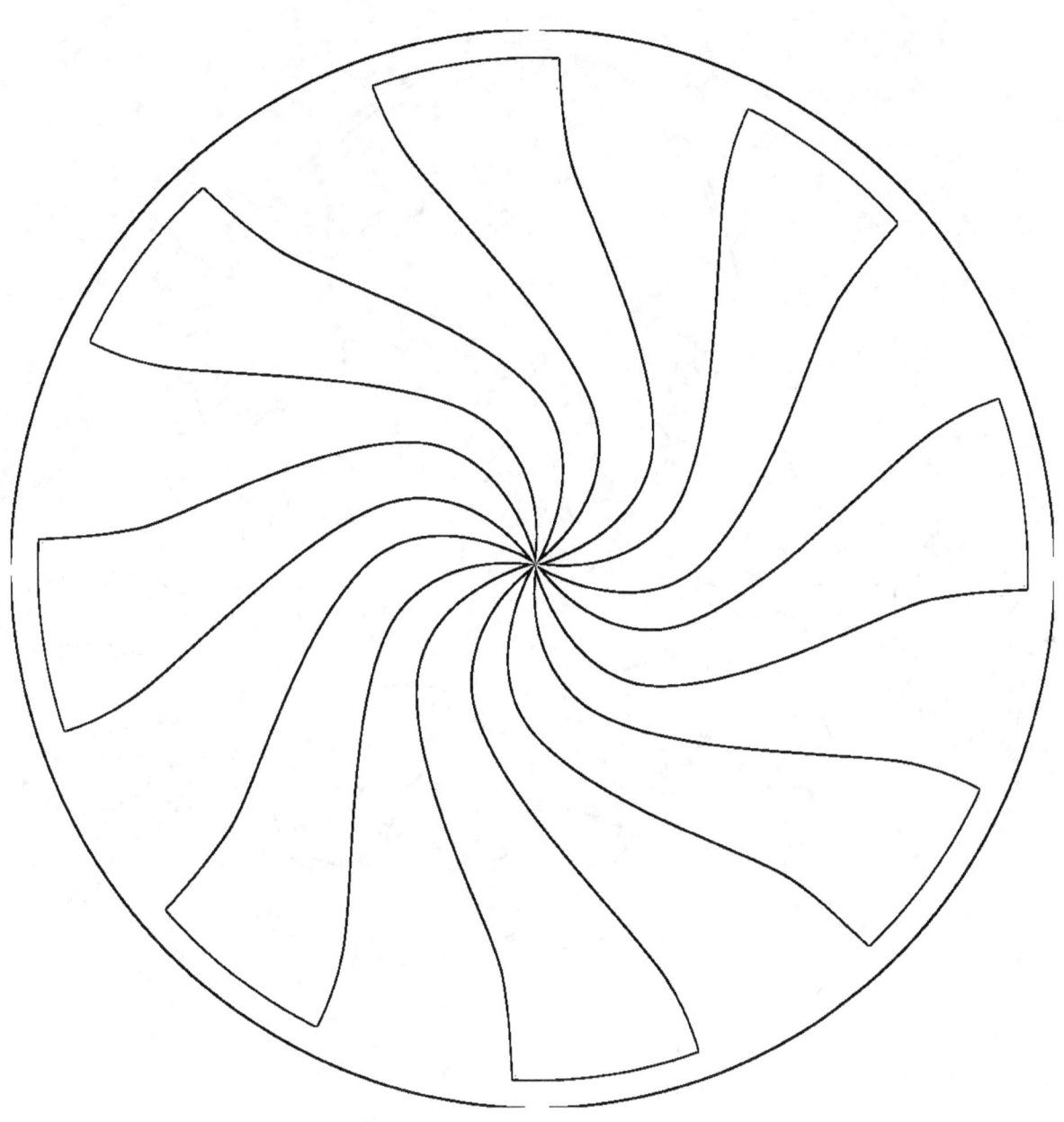

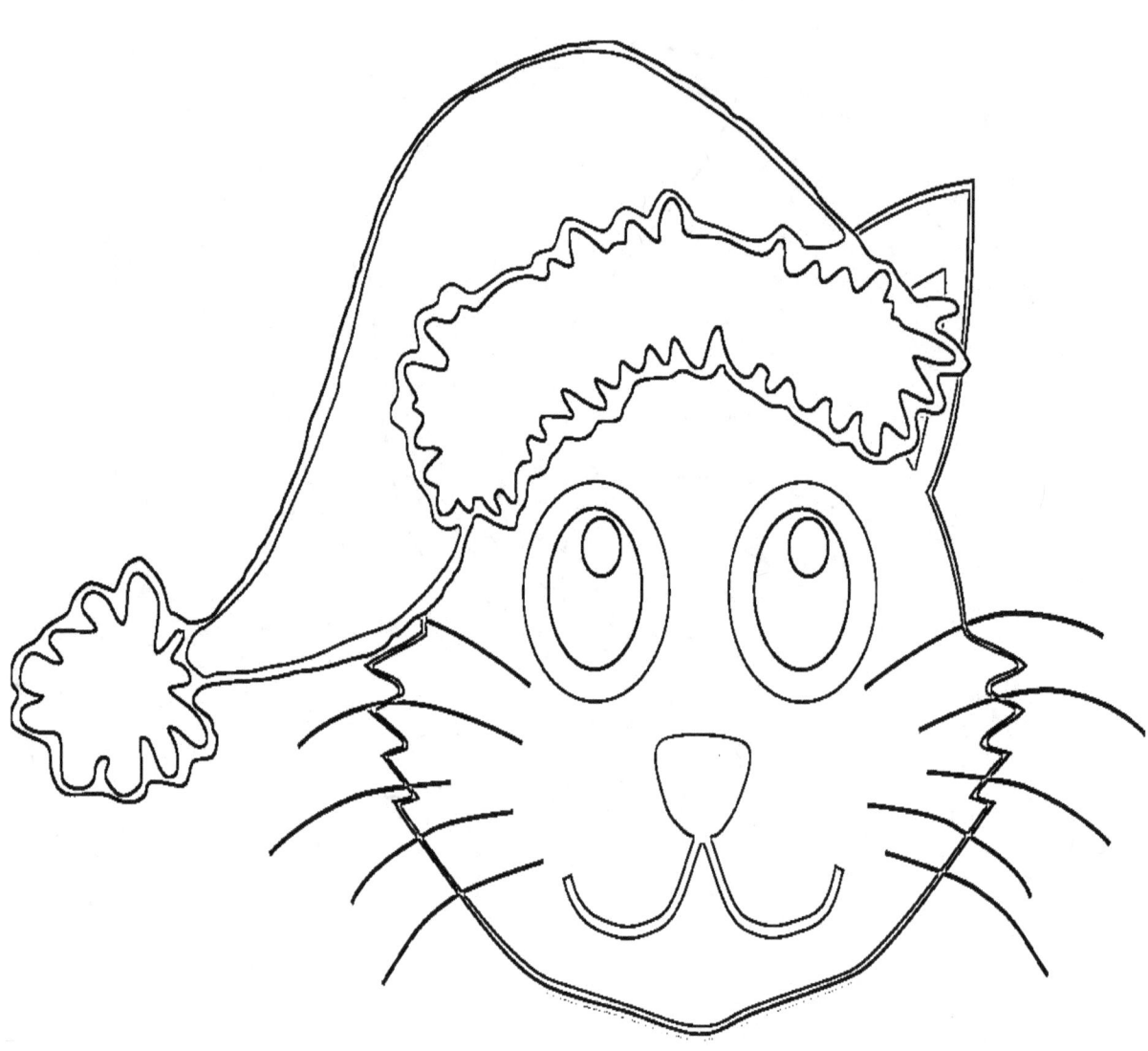

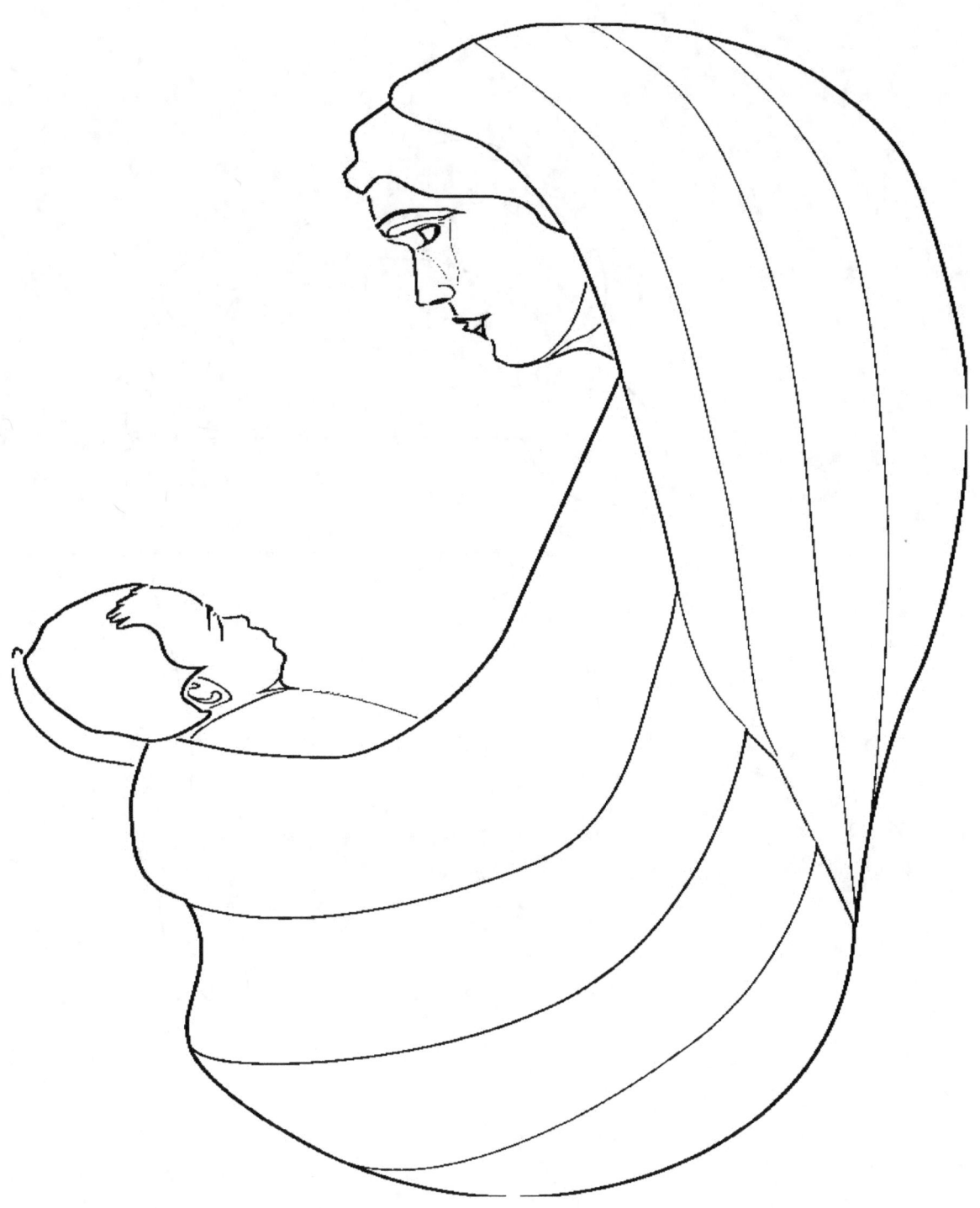

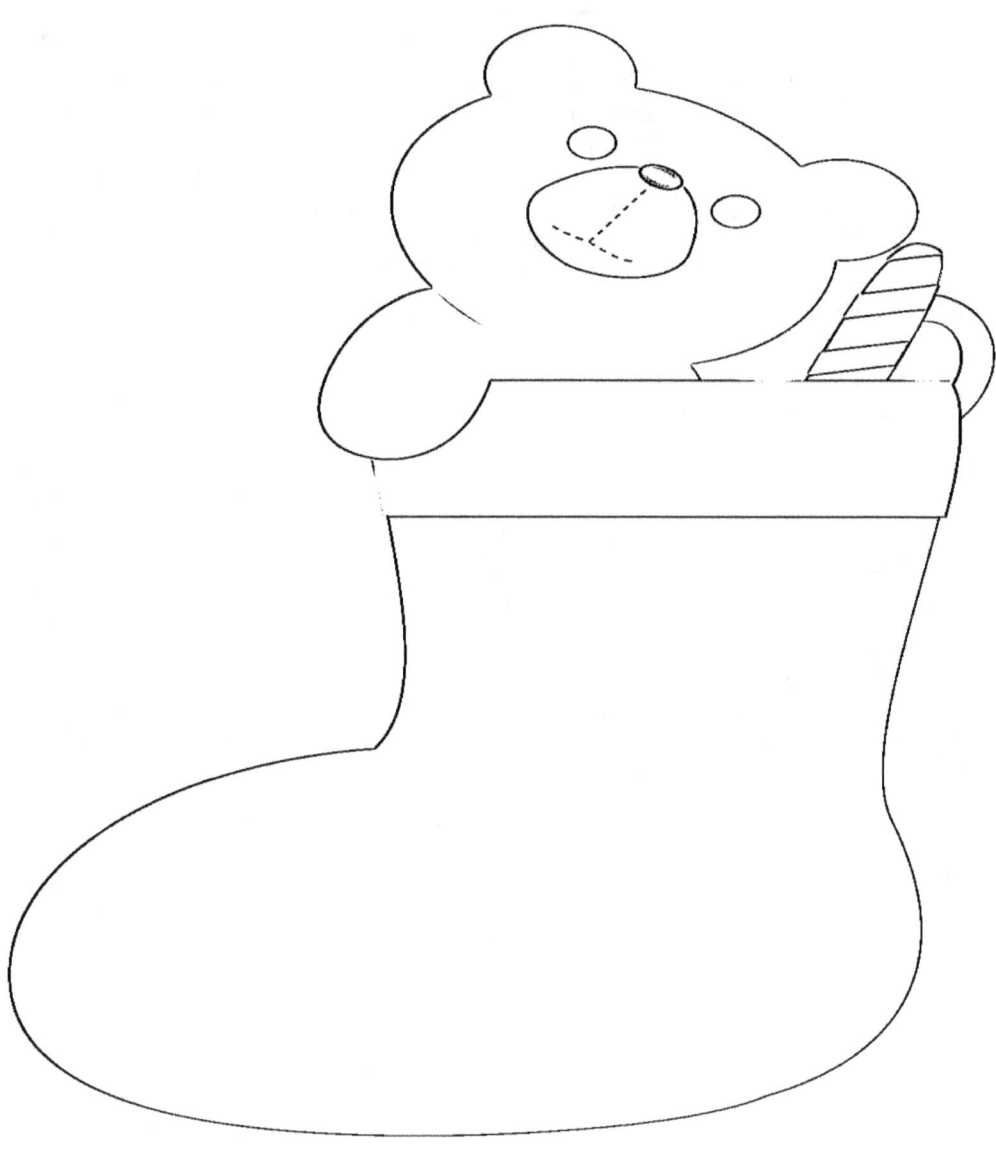

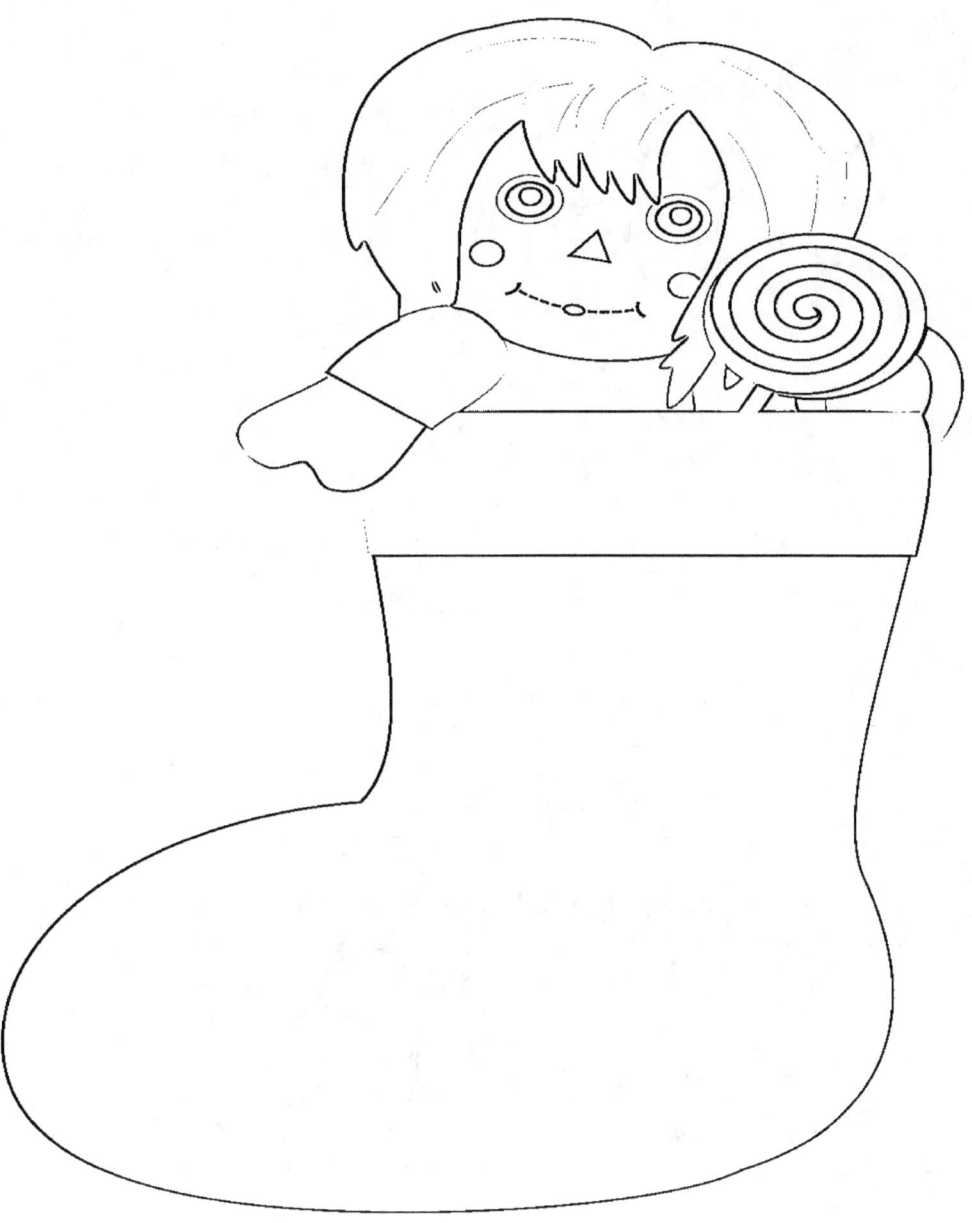

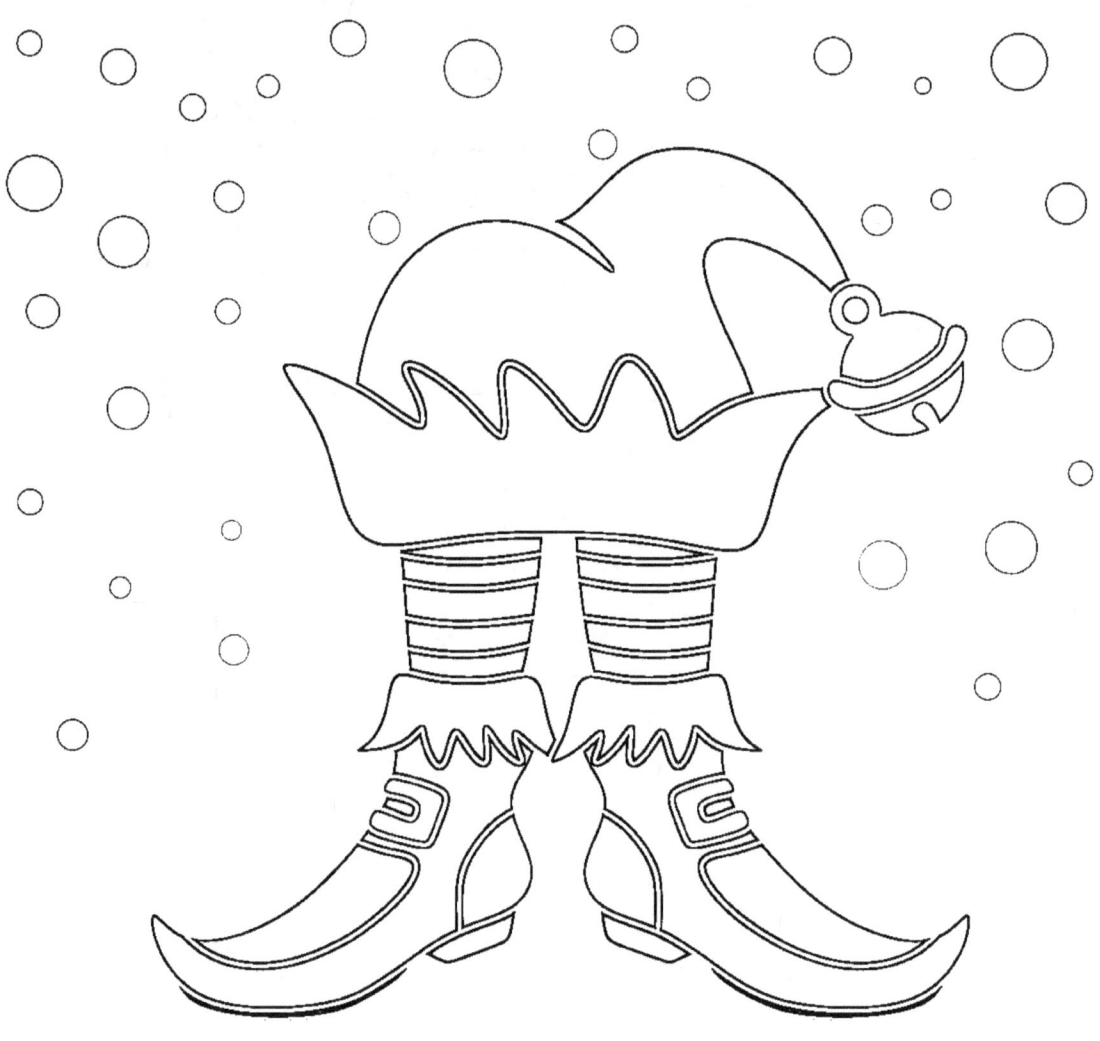

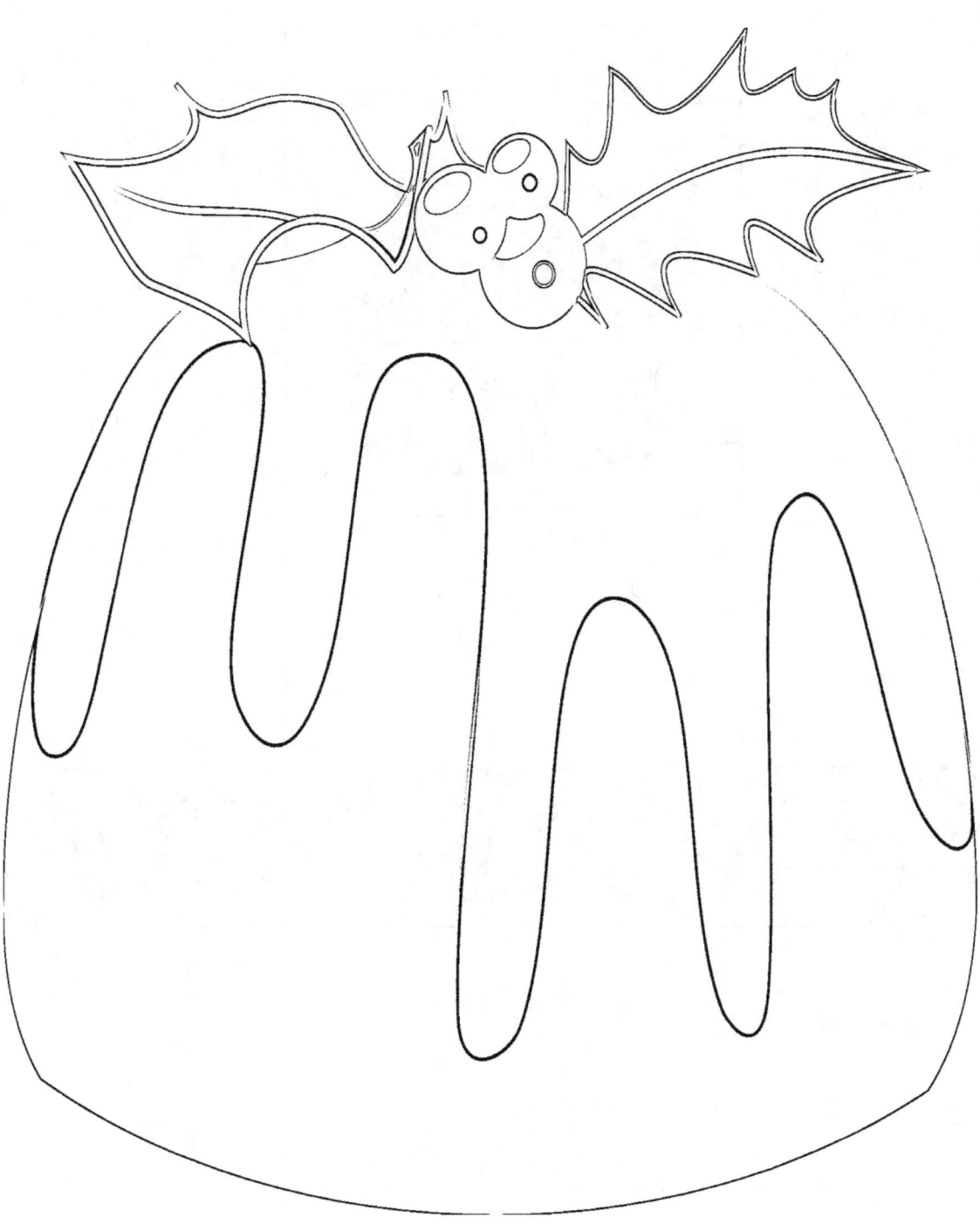

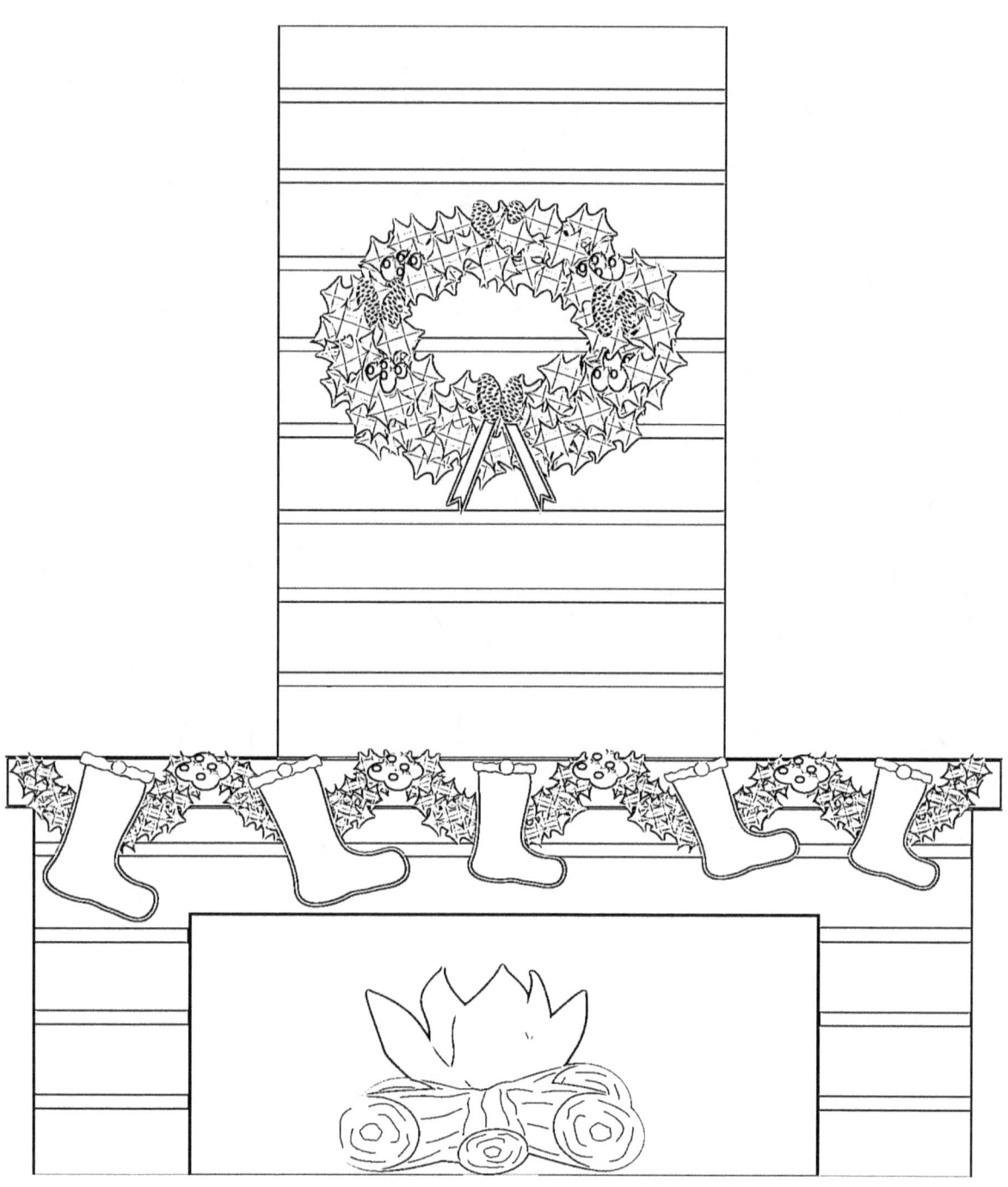

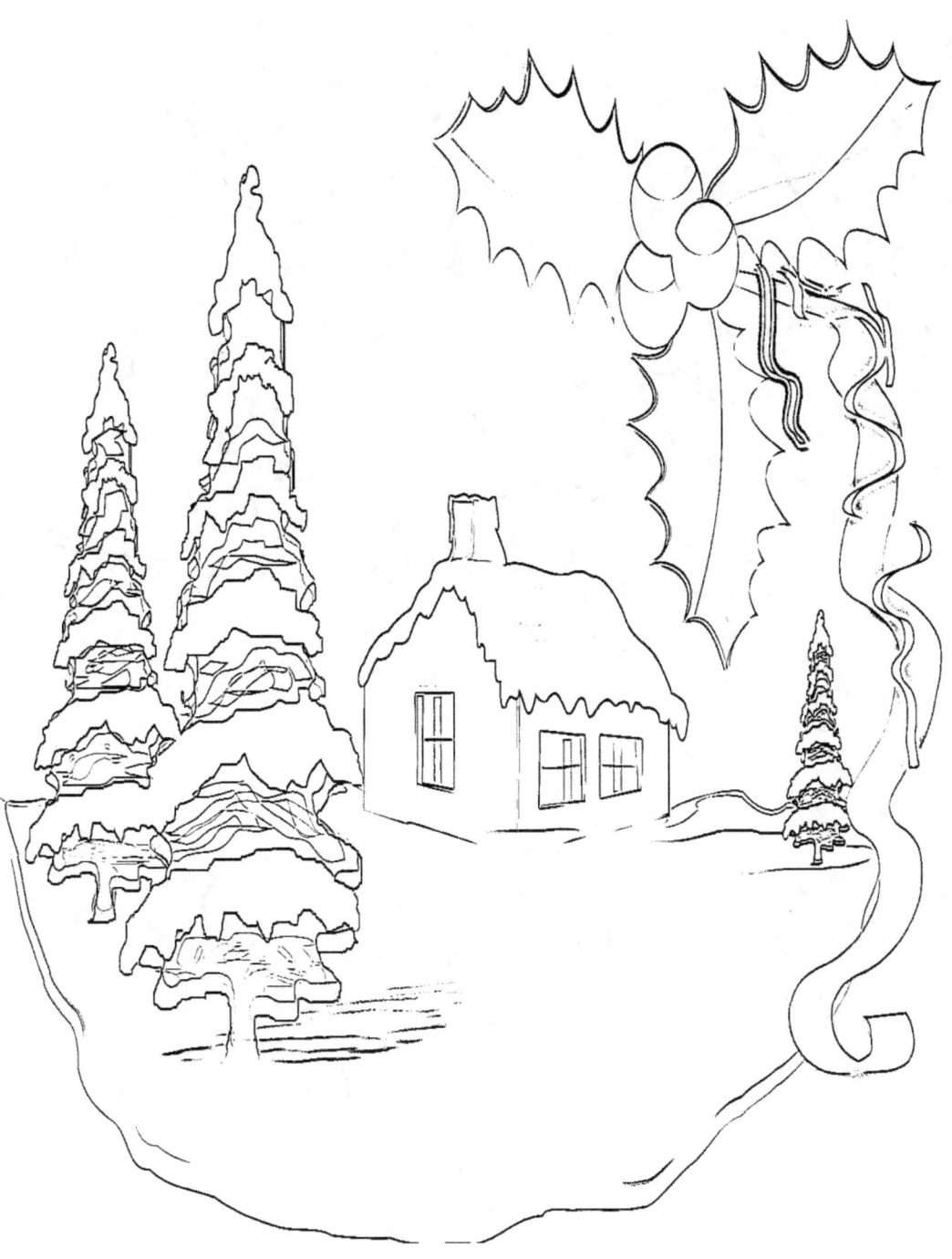

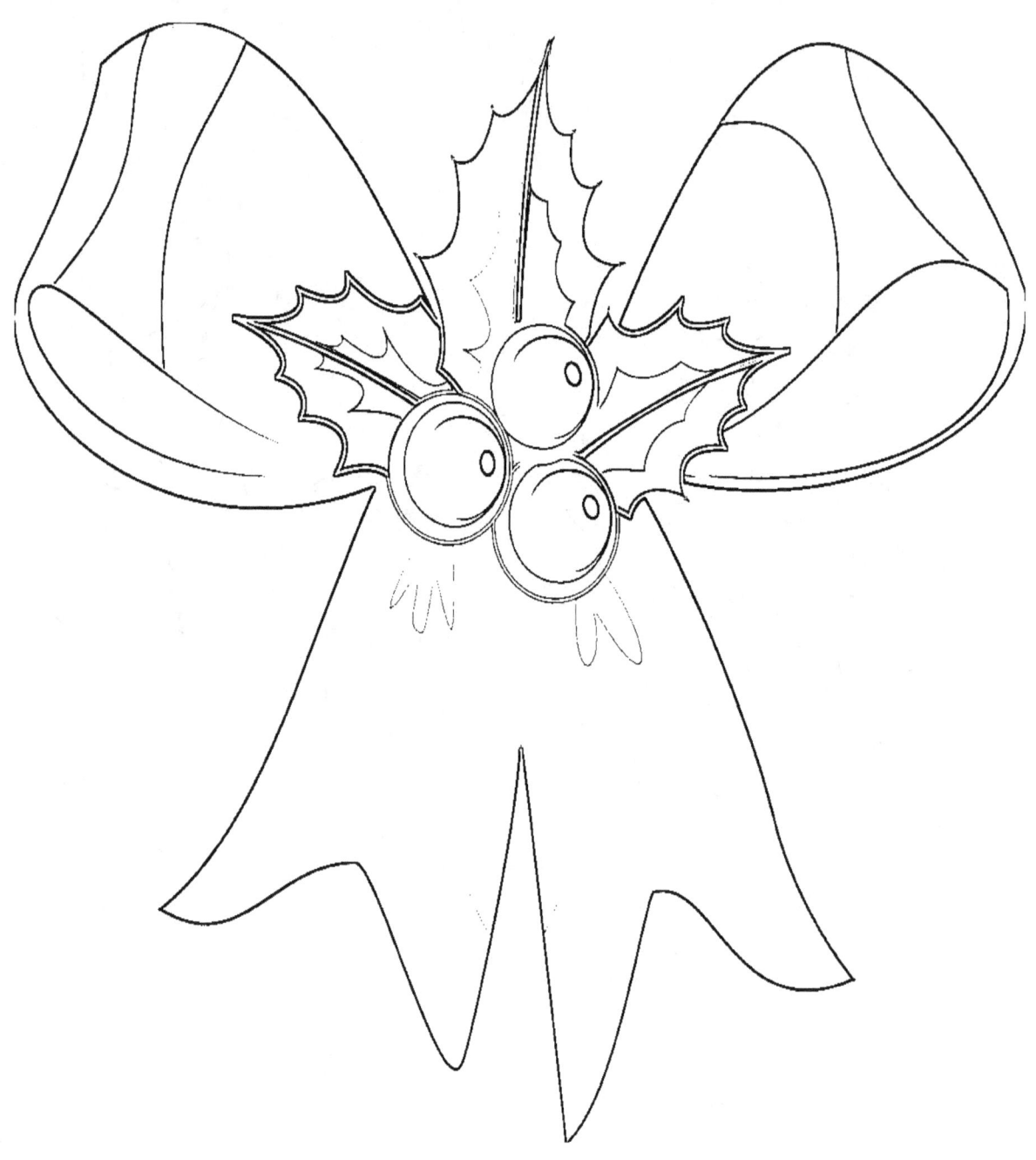

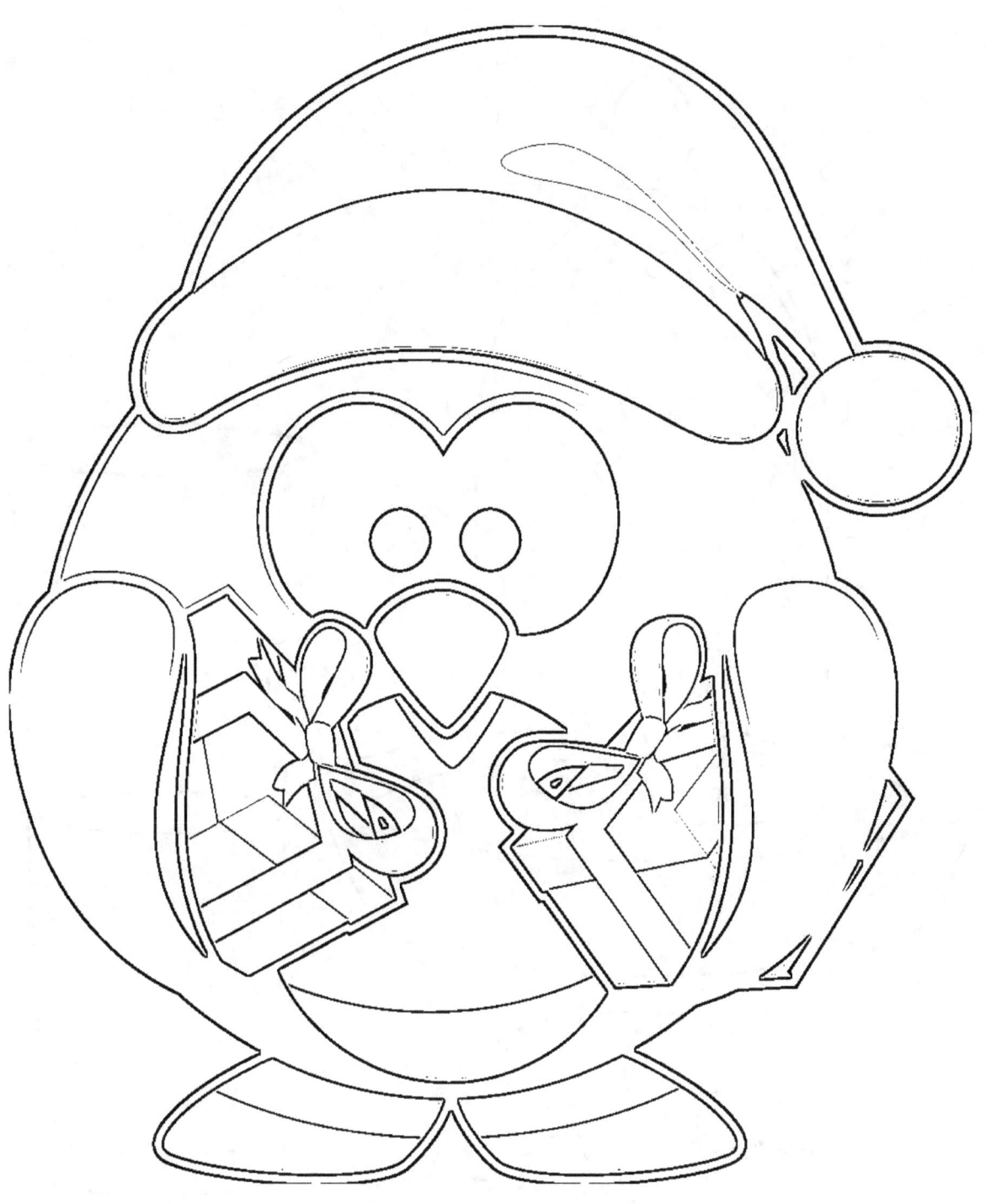

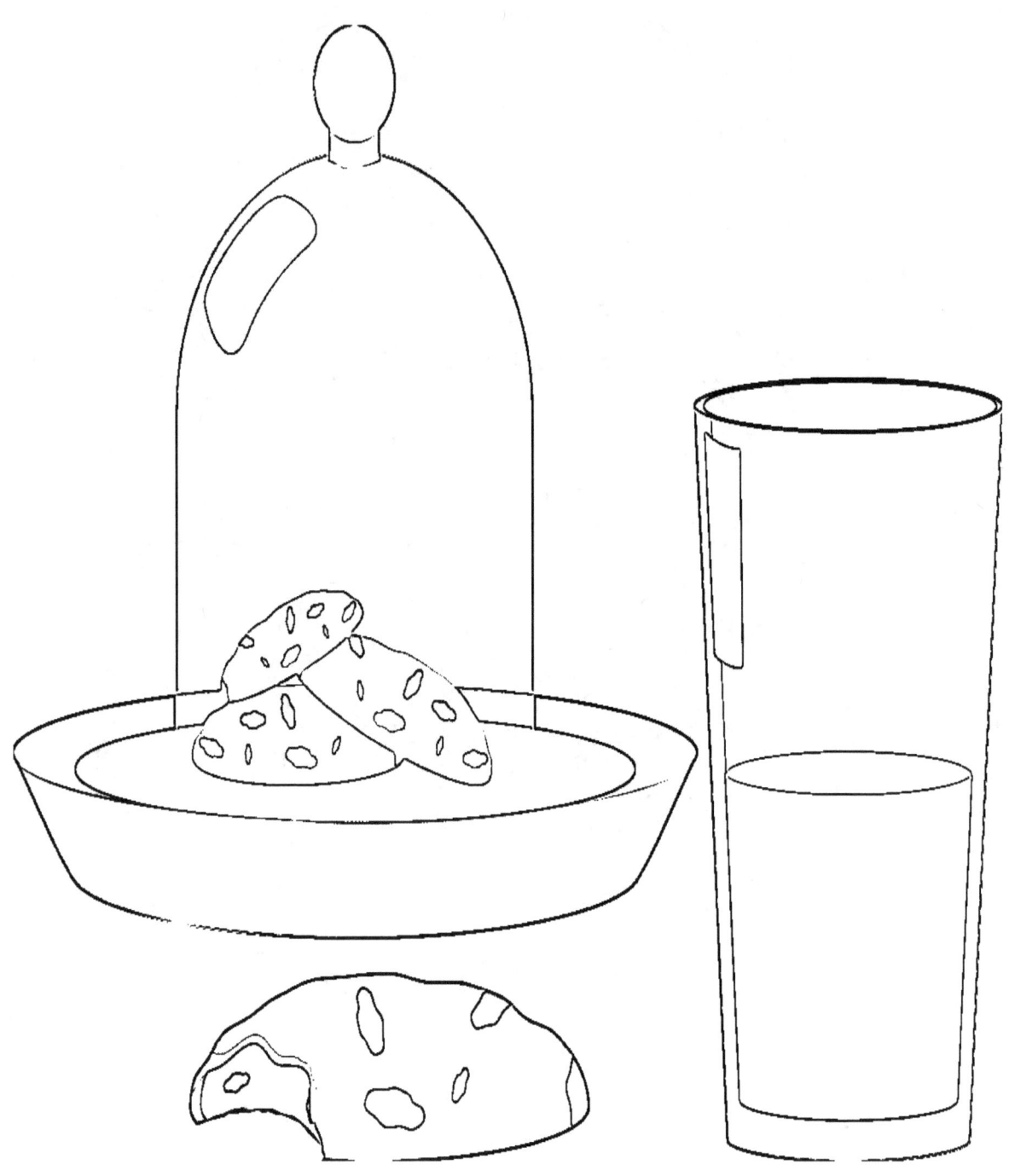

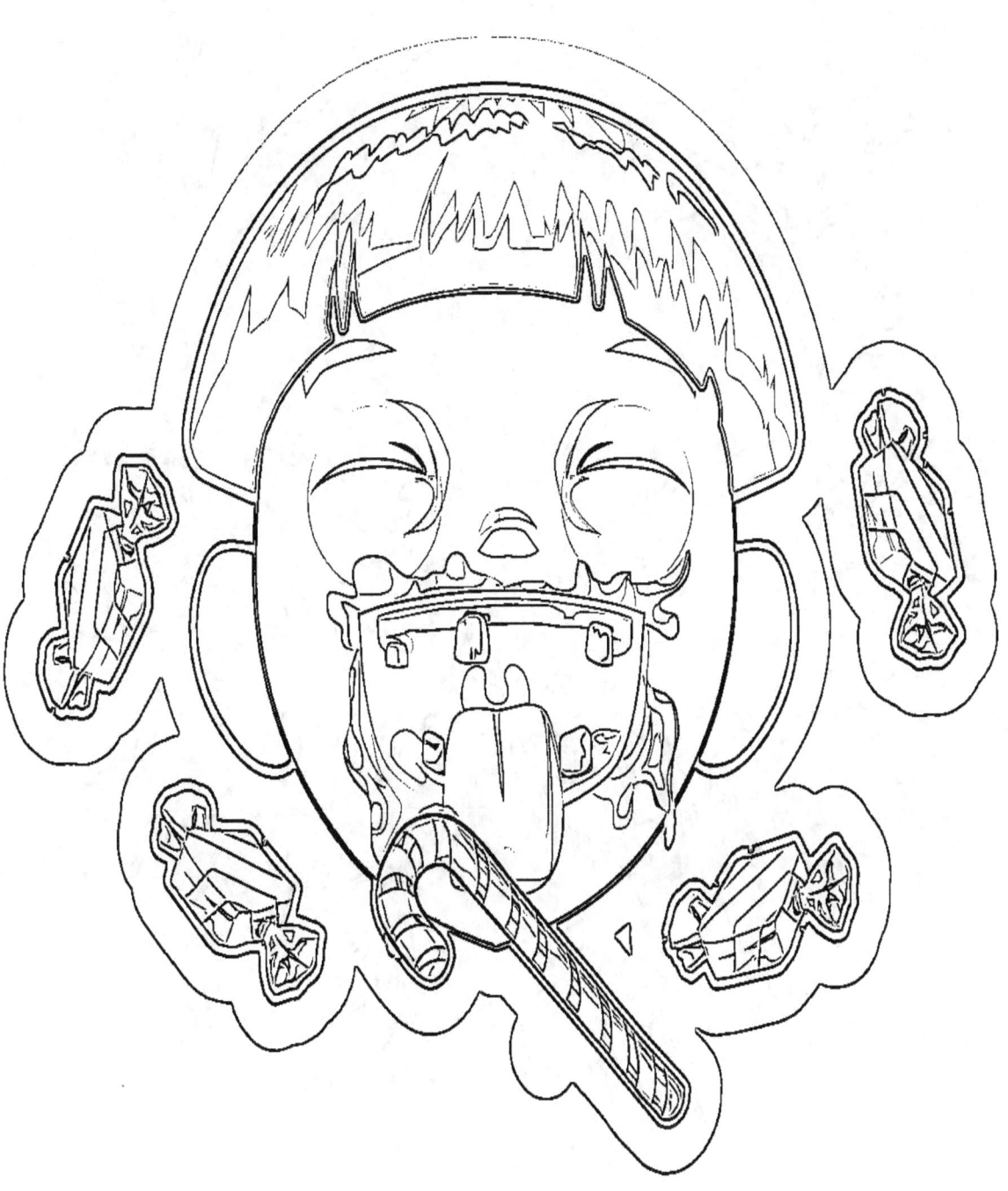

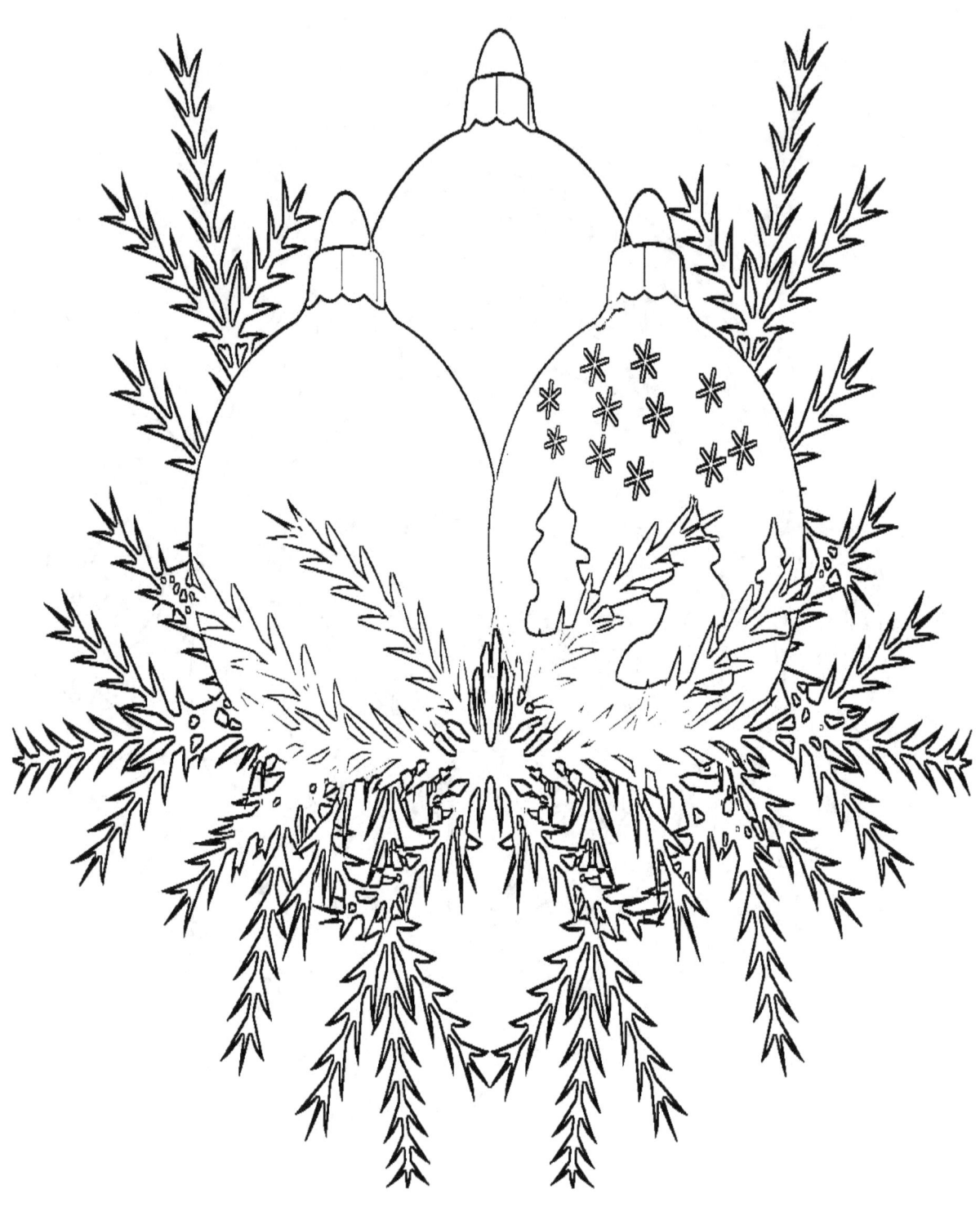

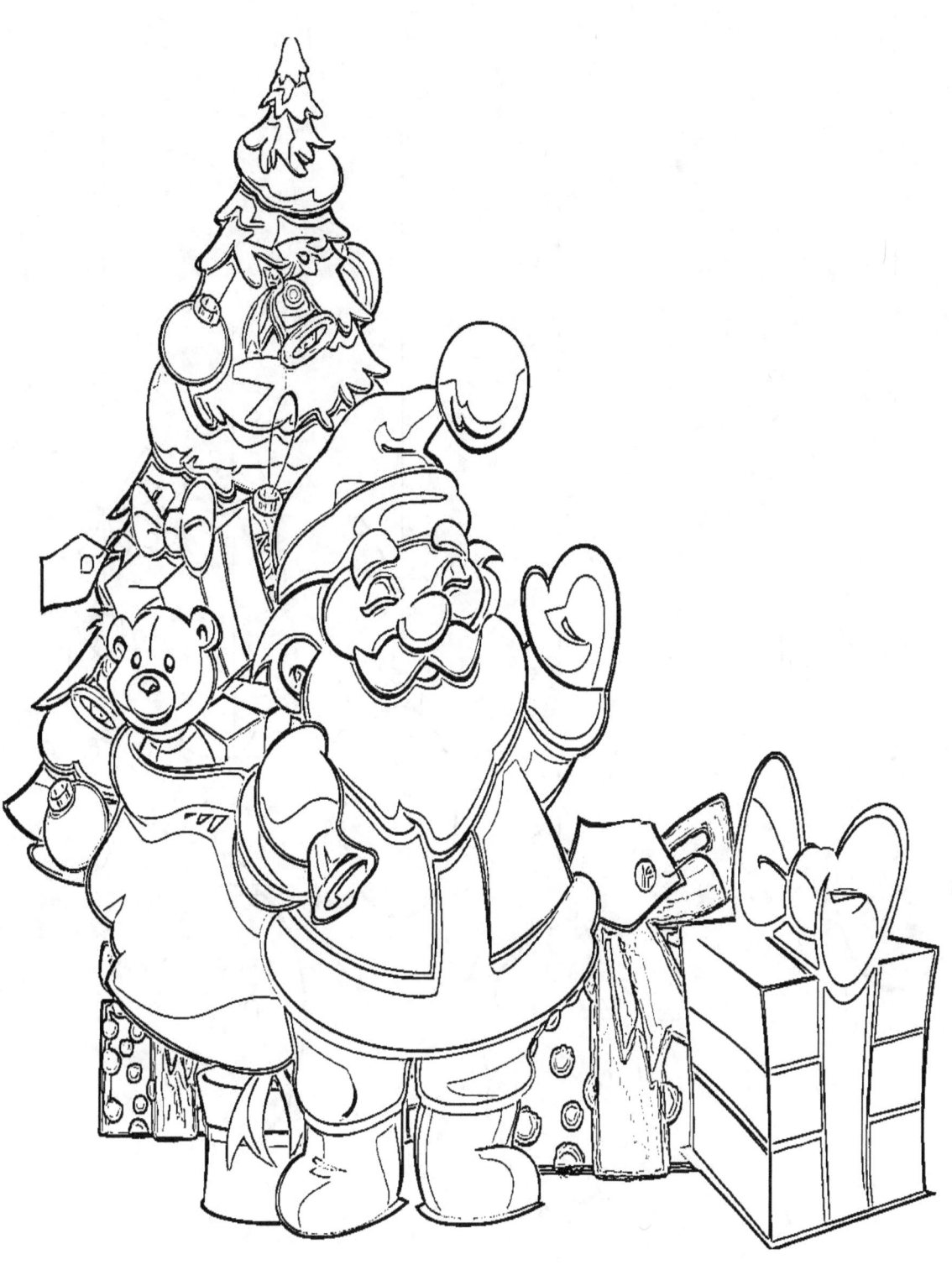

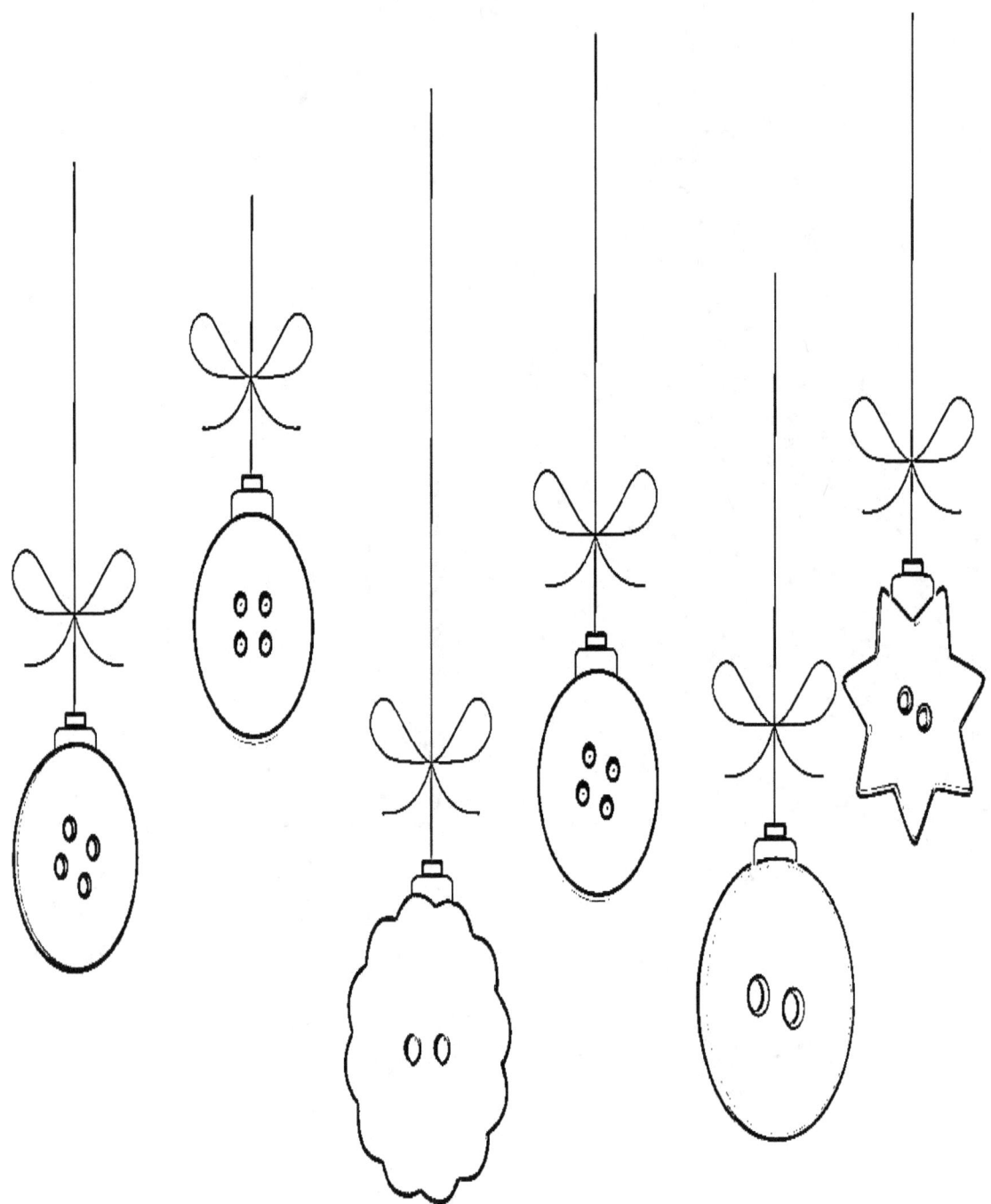

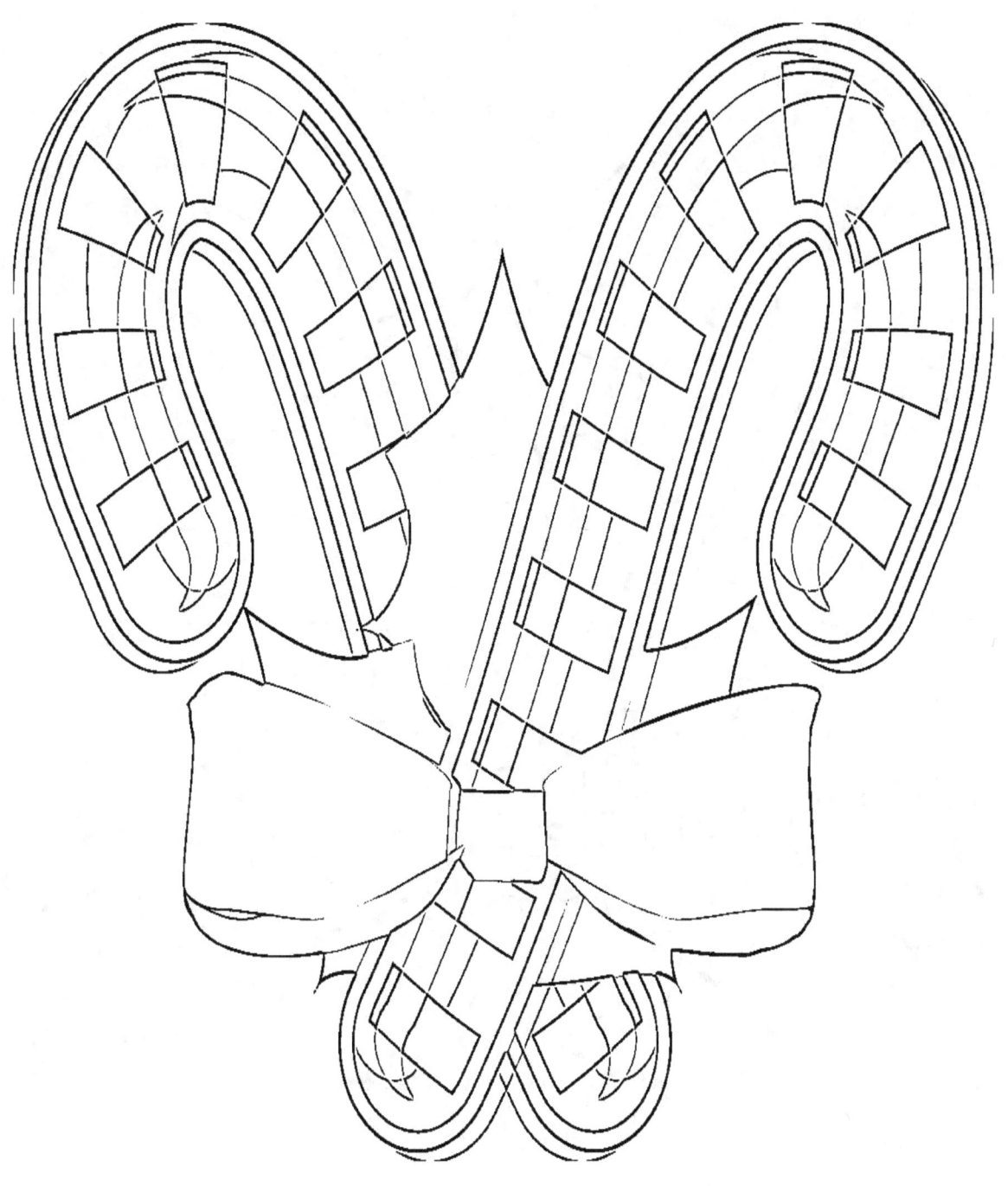

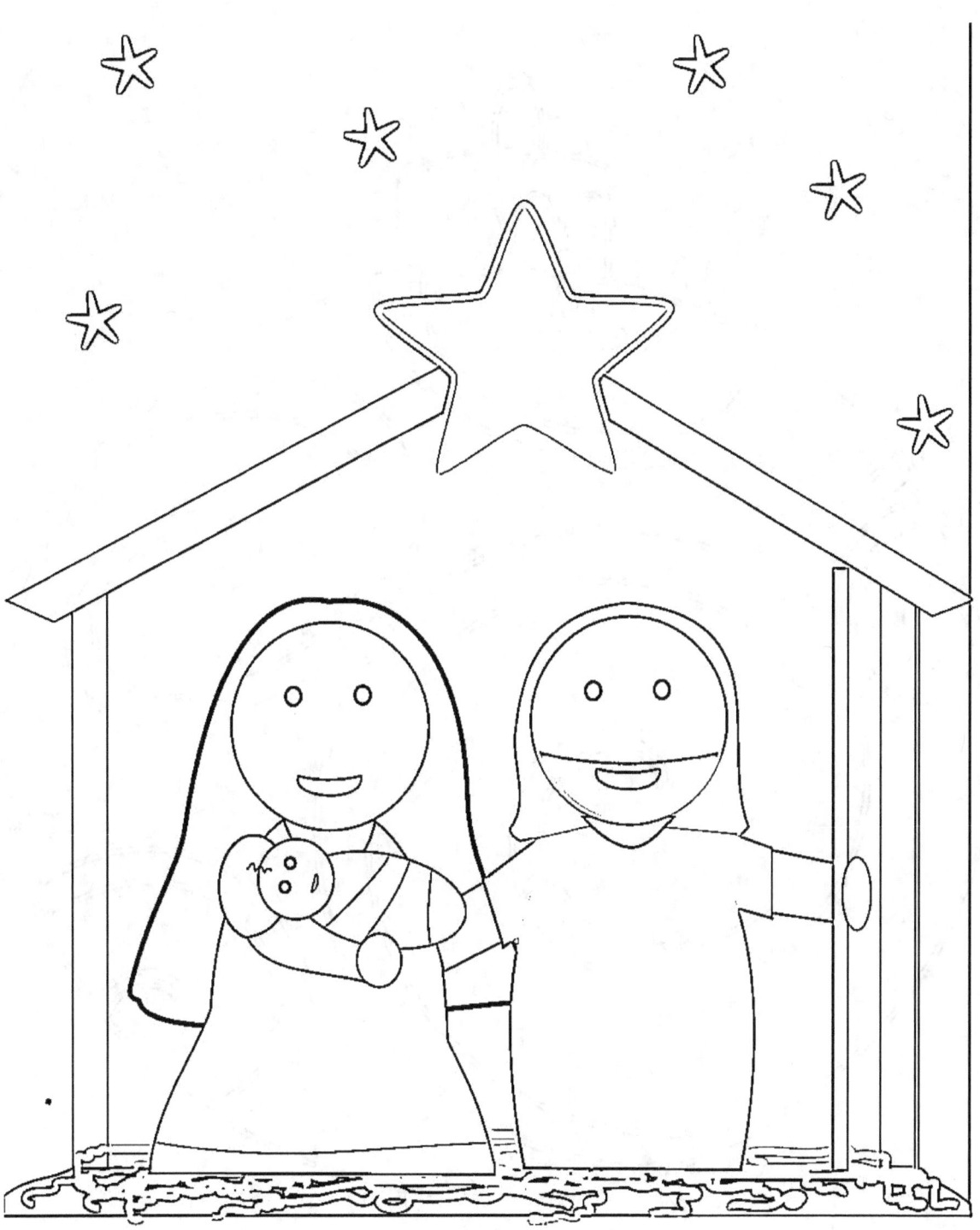

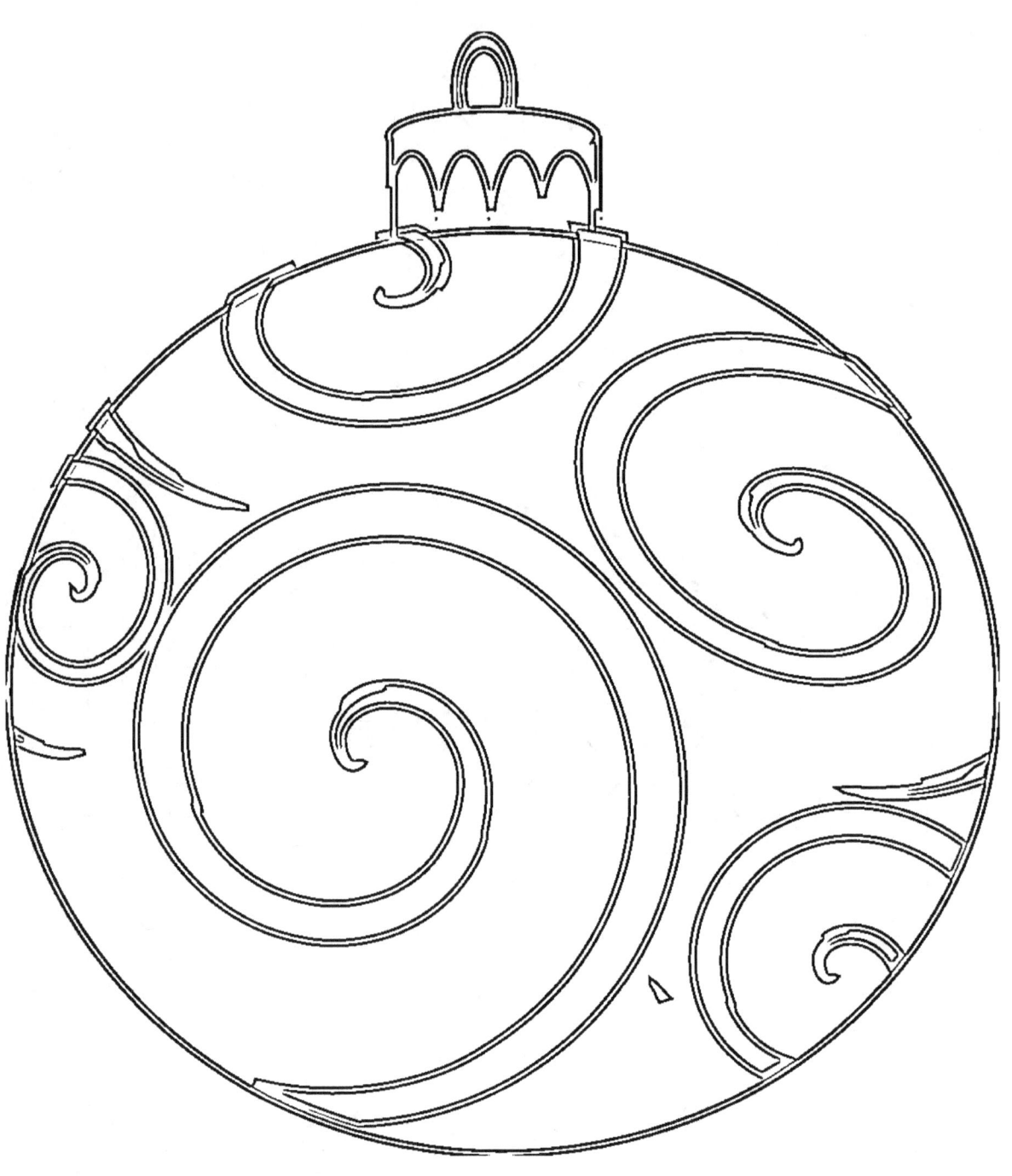

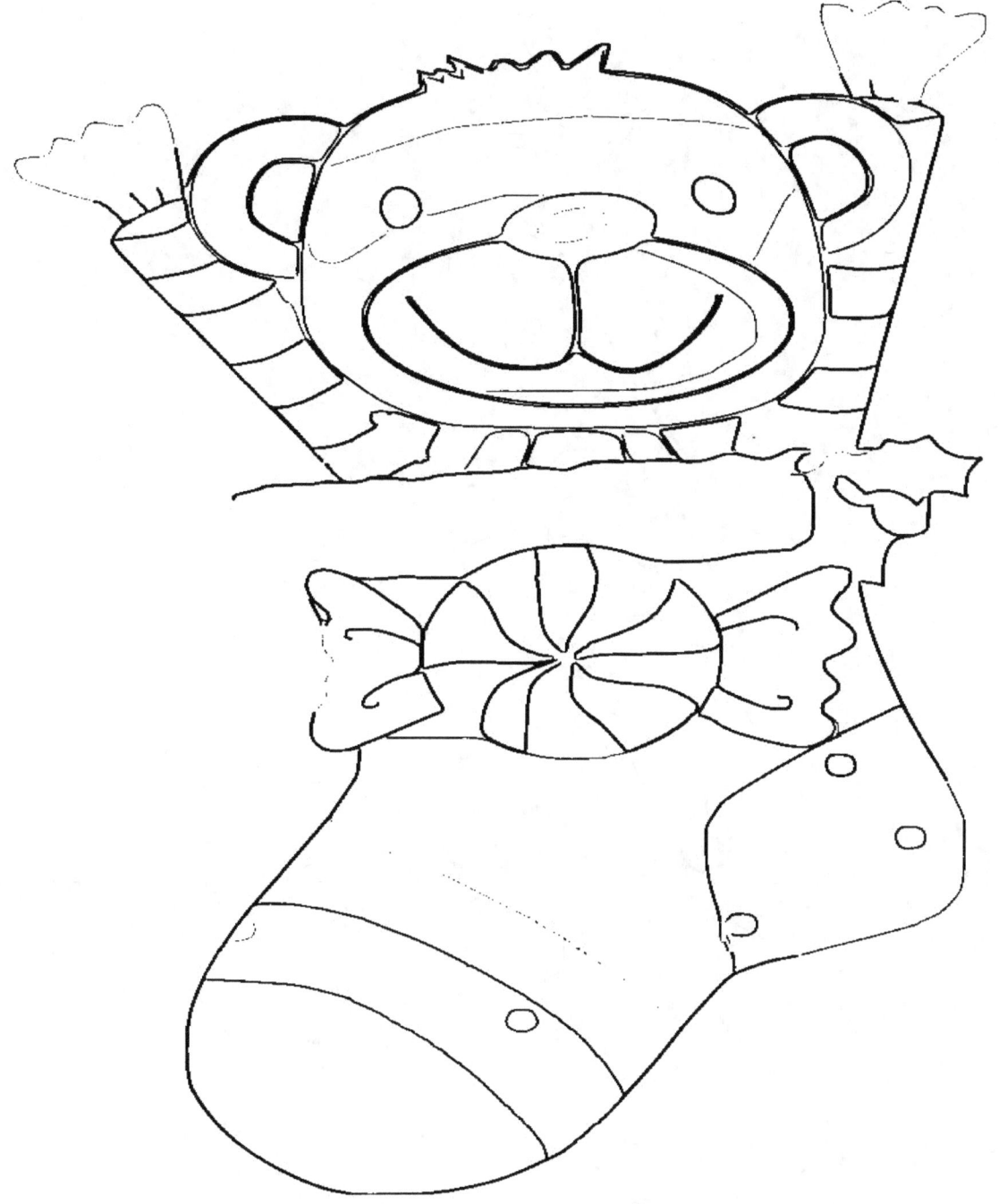

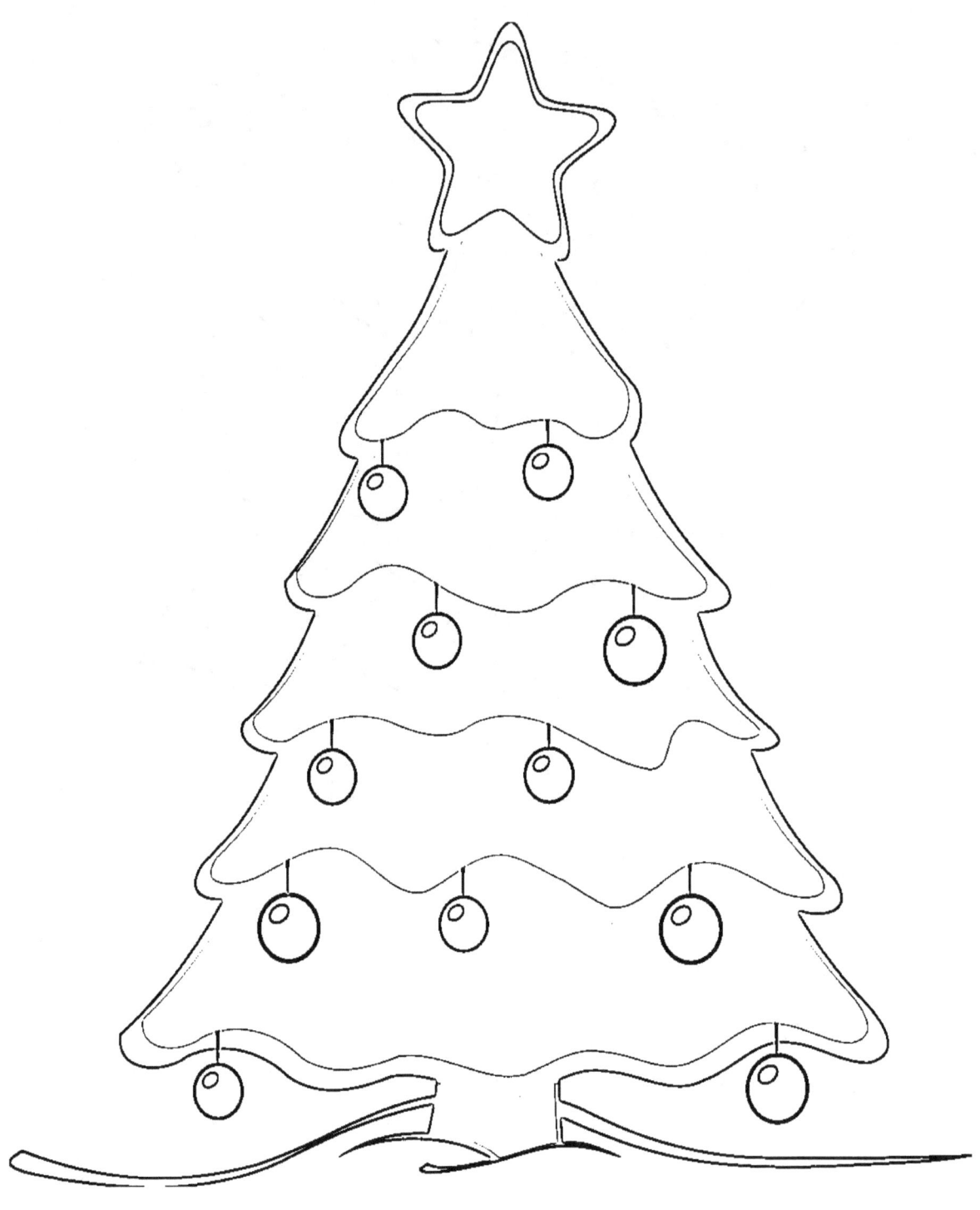

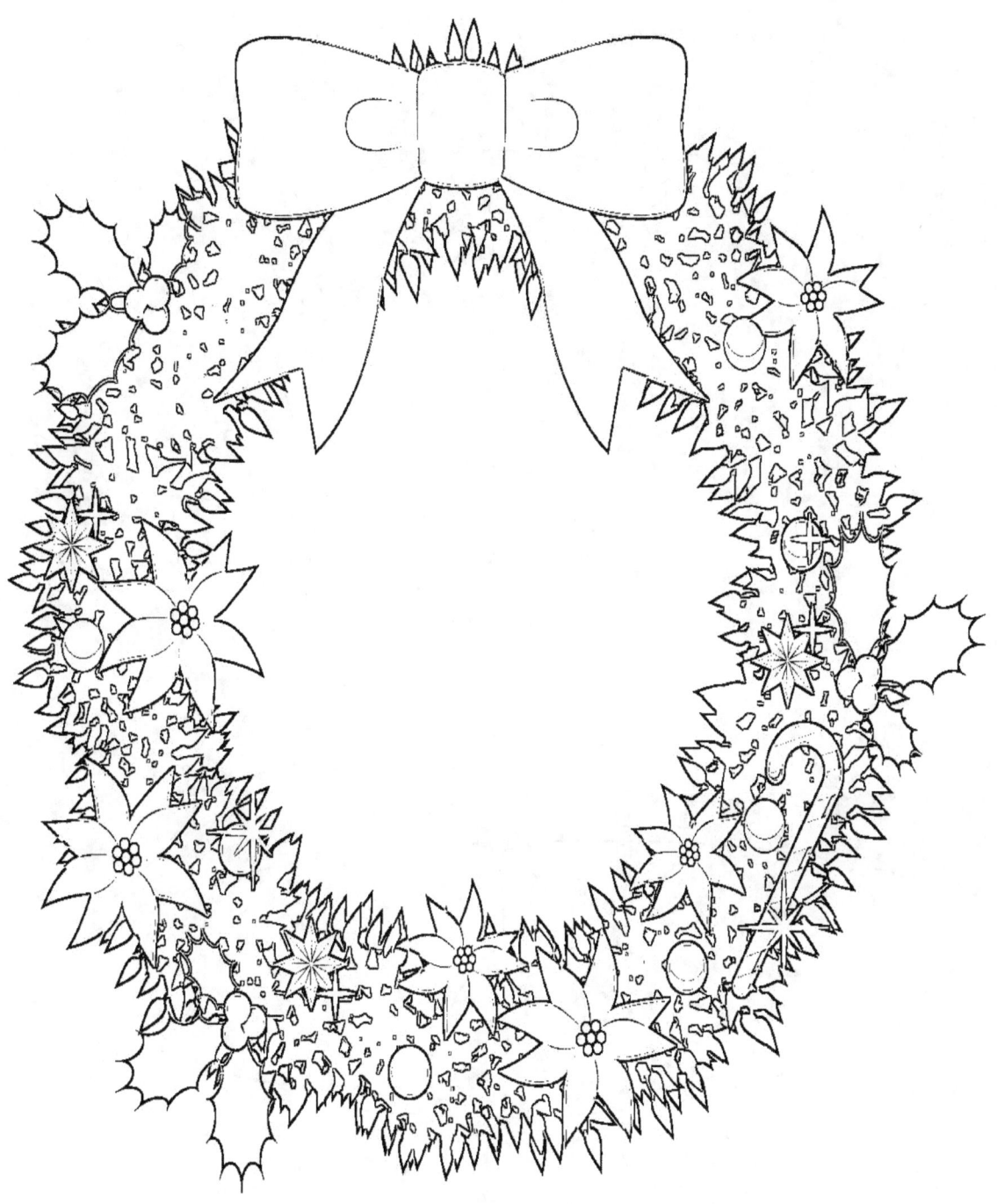

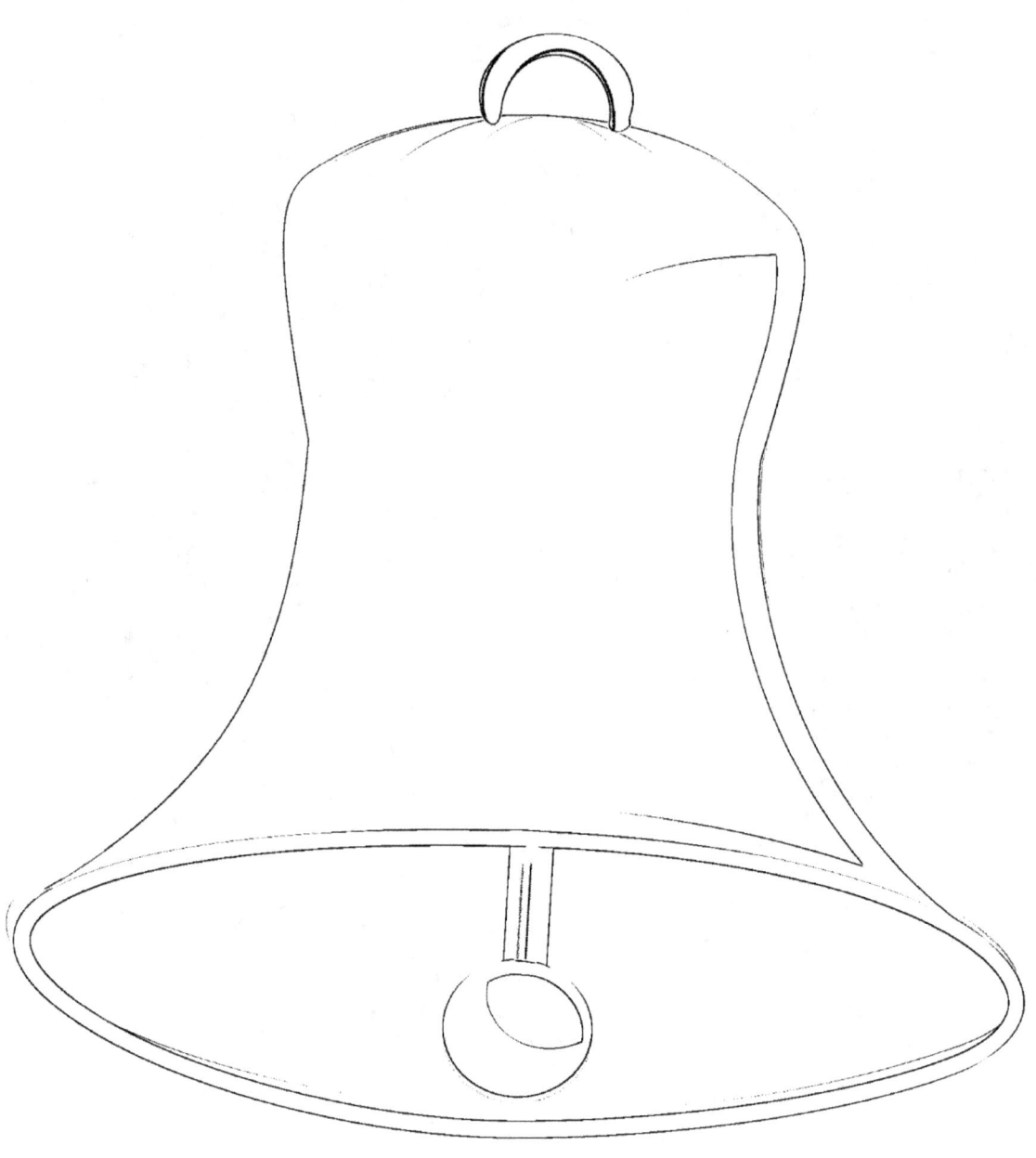

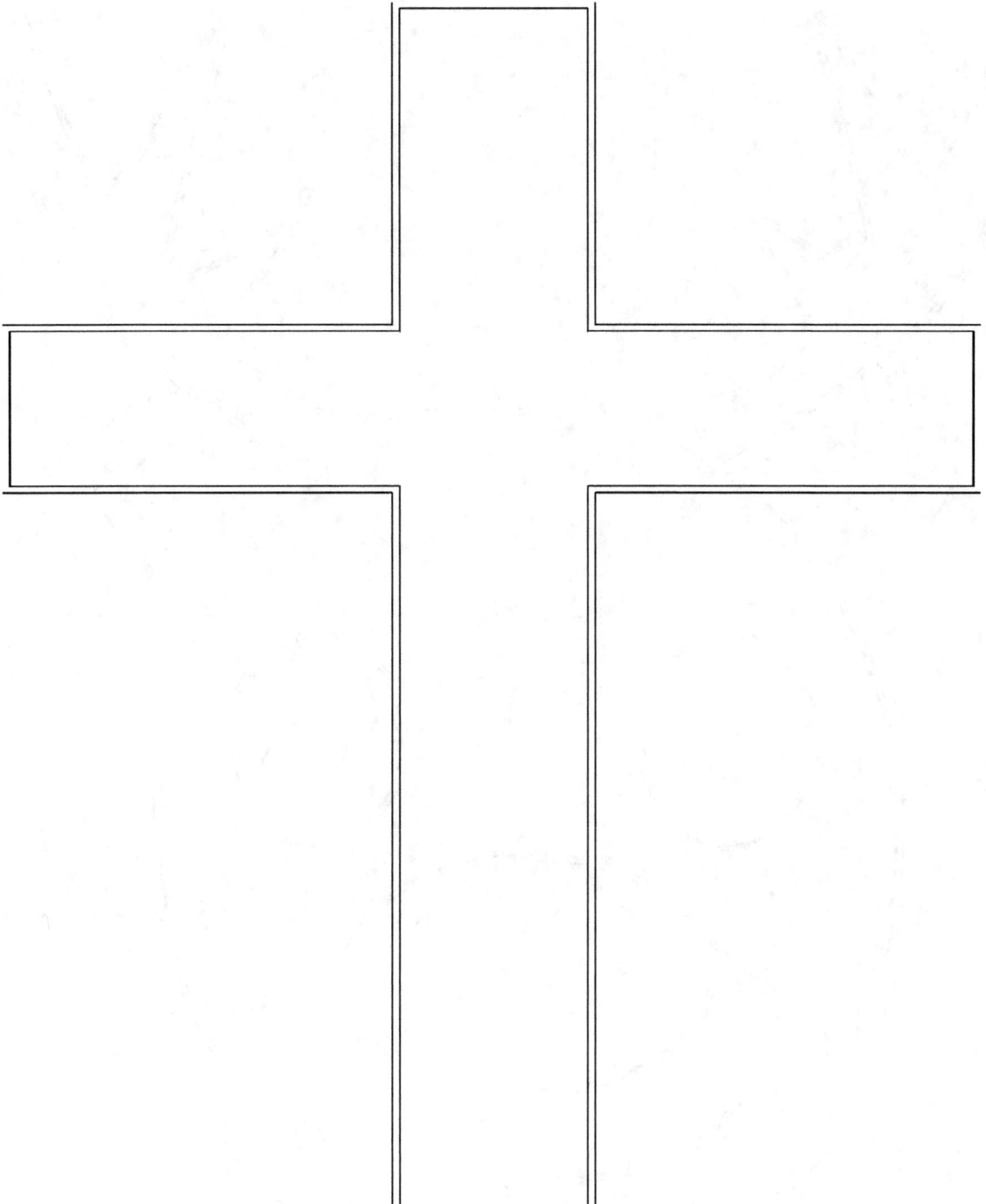

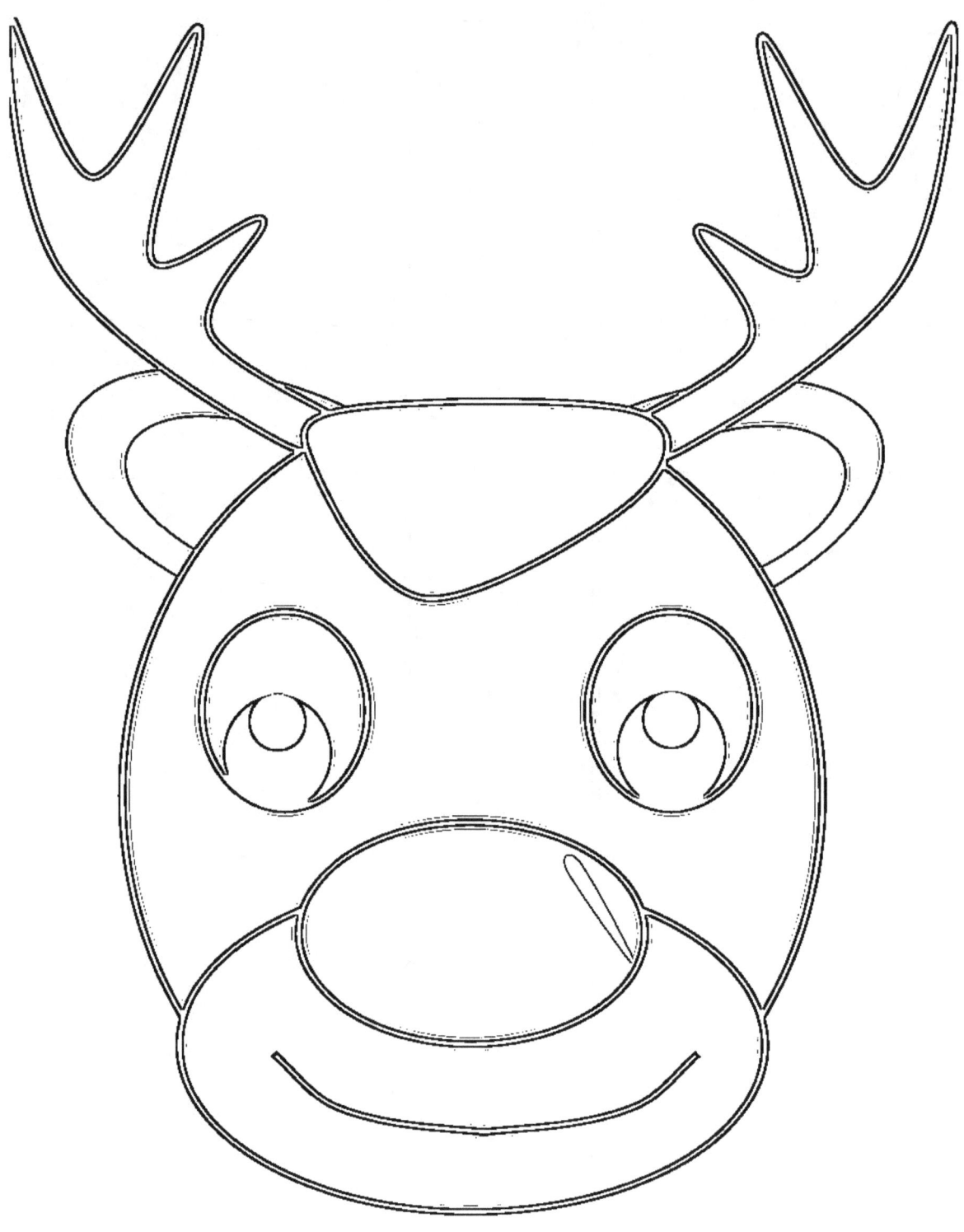

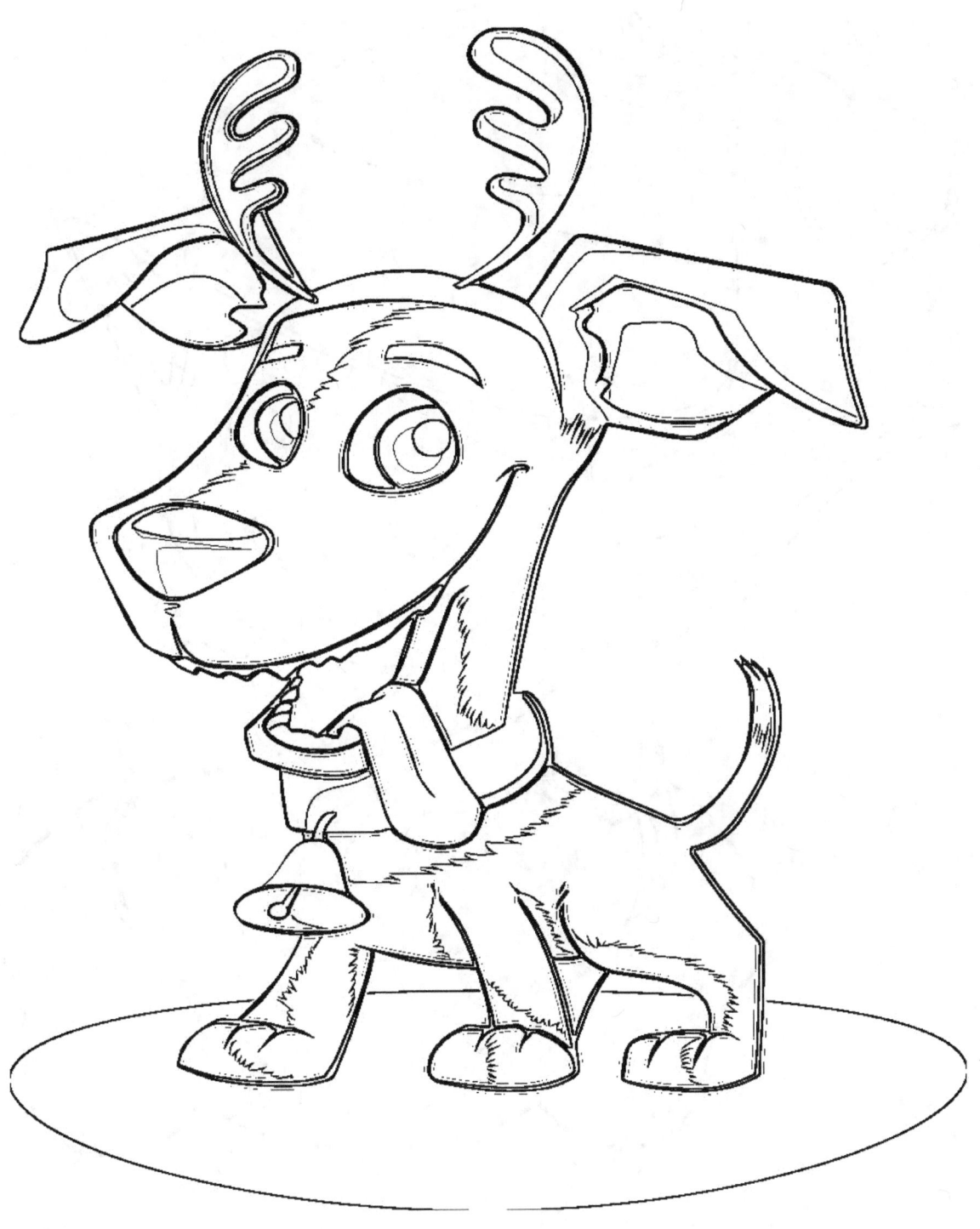

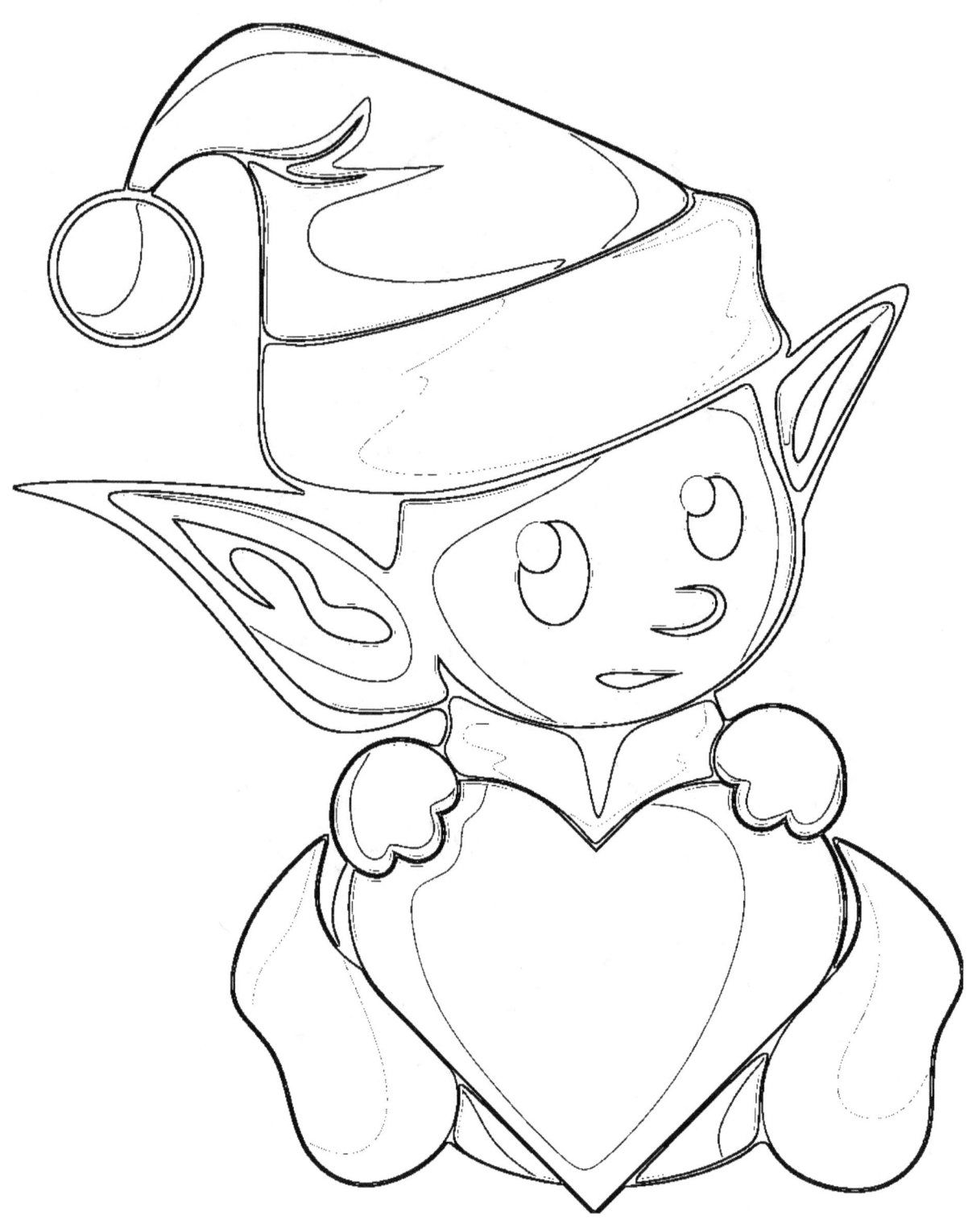

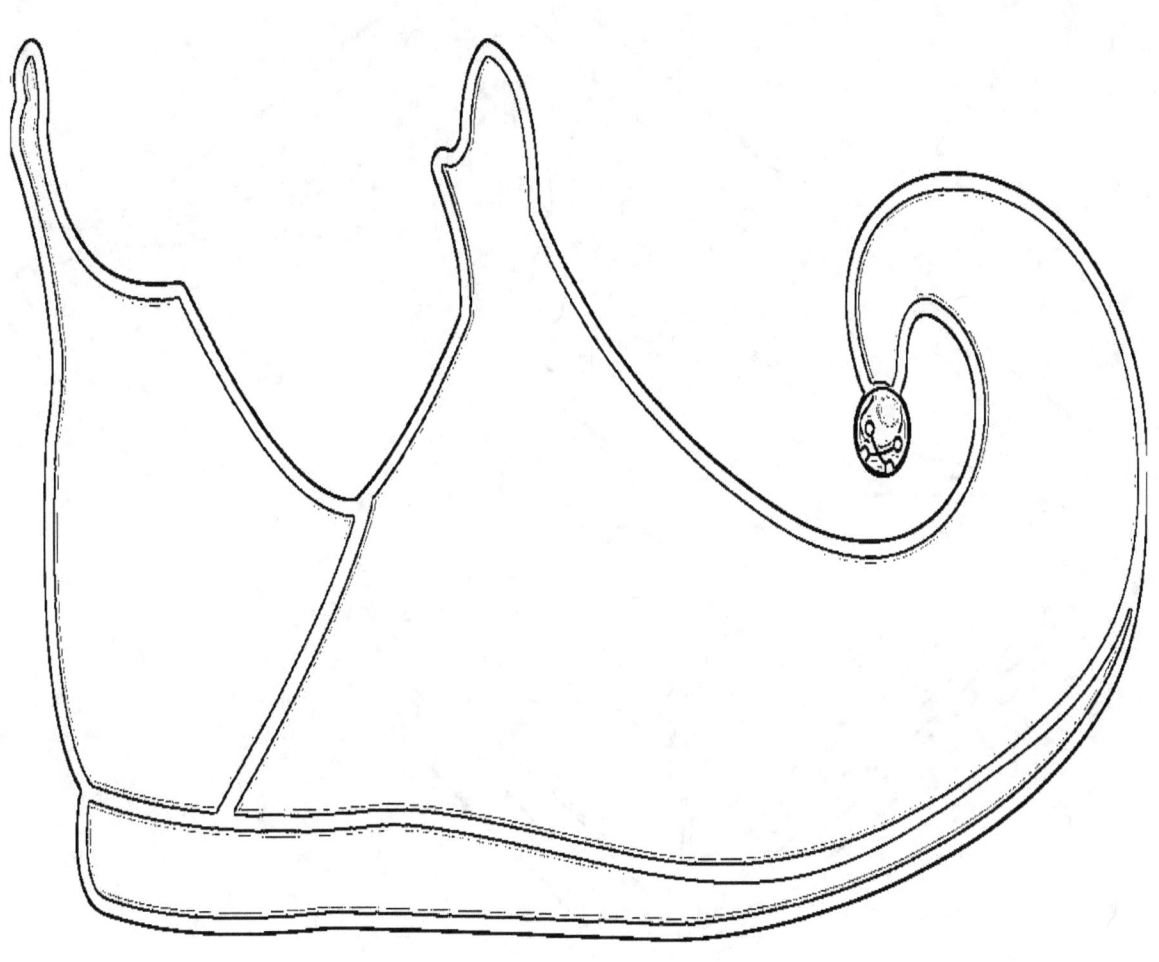

A Christmas Card For Santa:

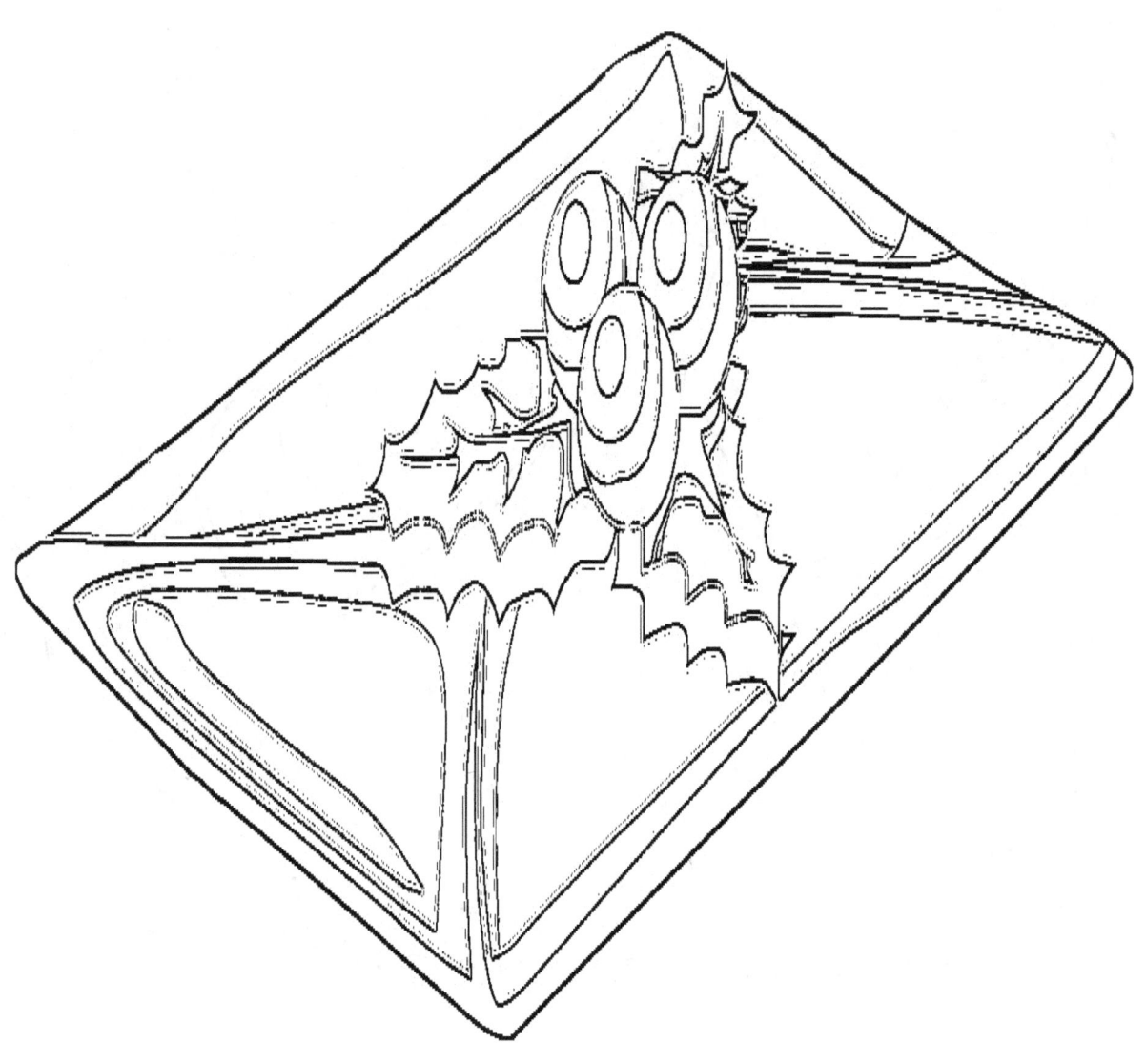

From Me And "Elfie"

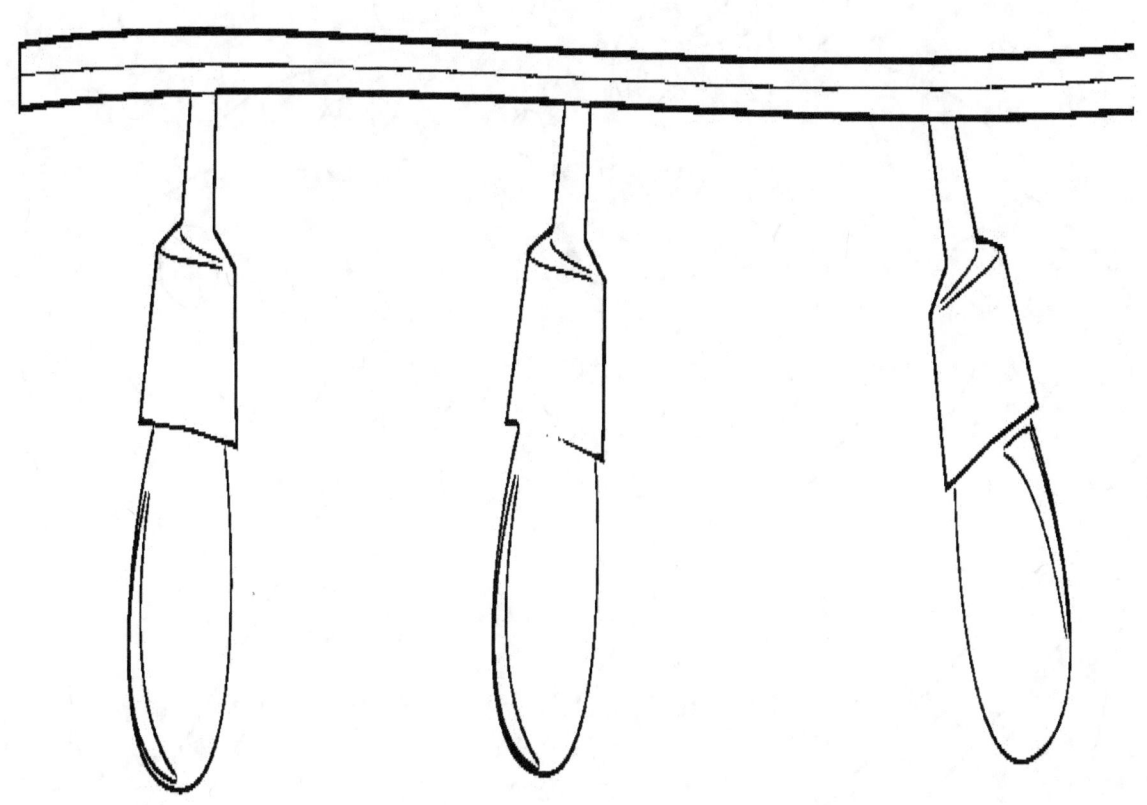

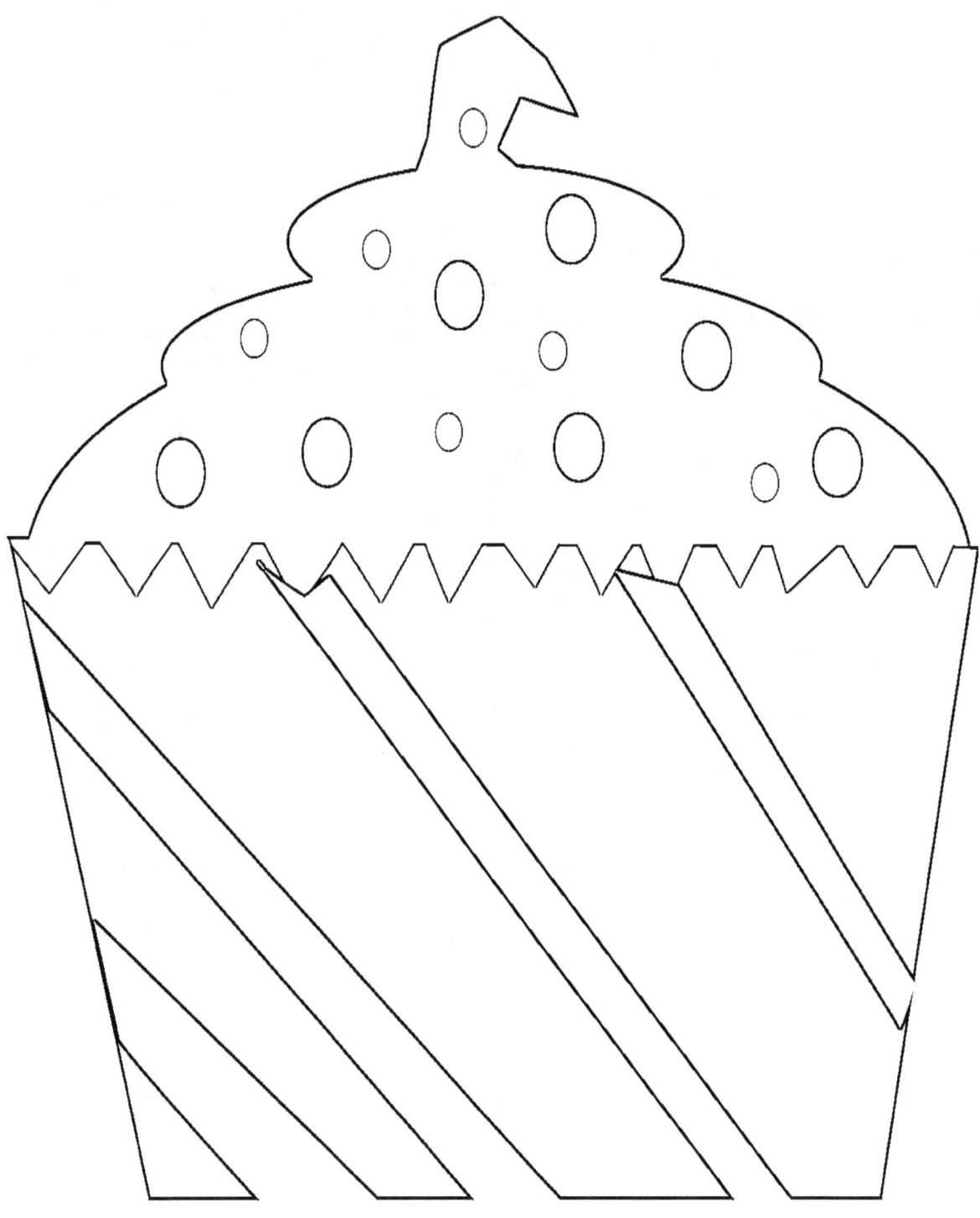

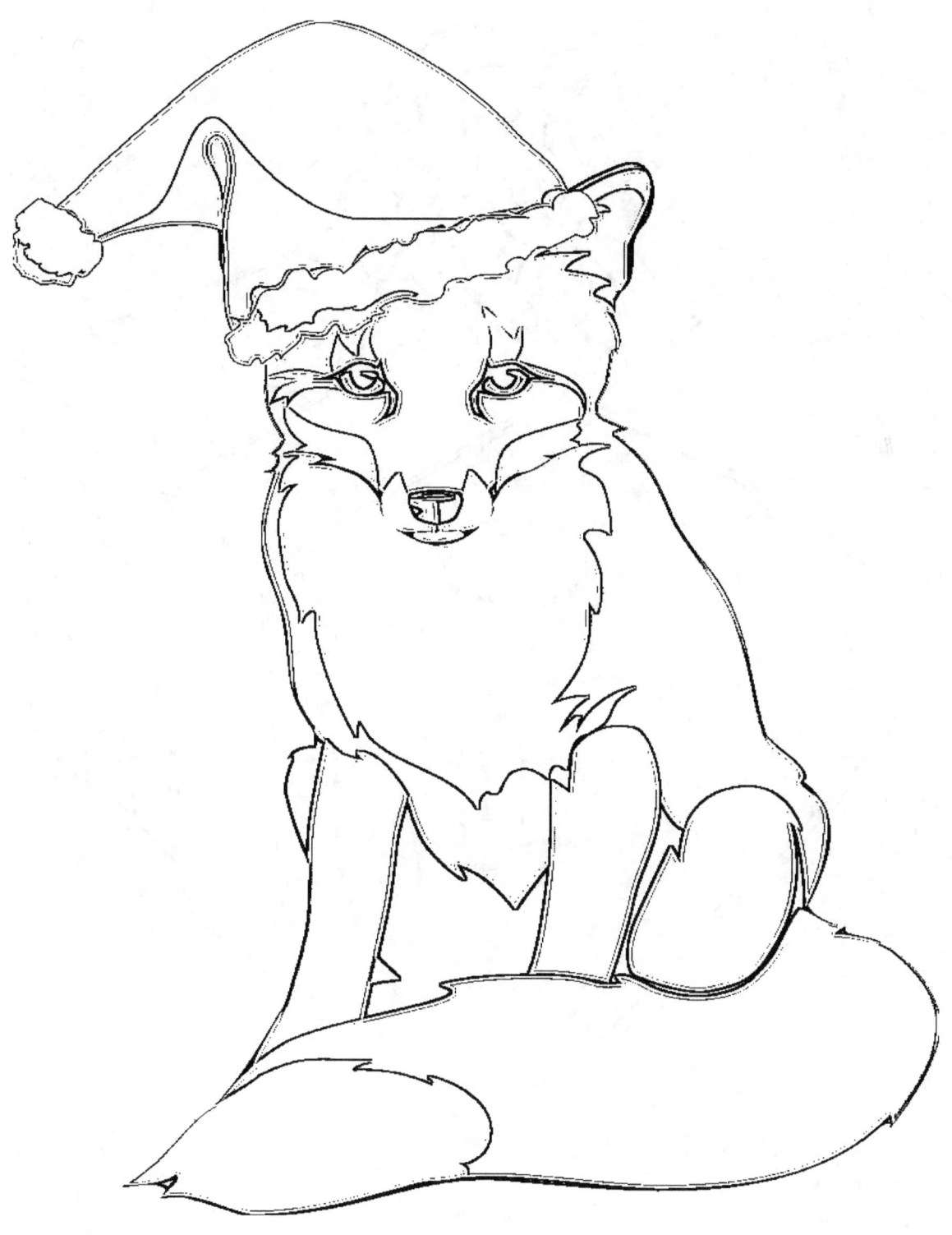

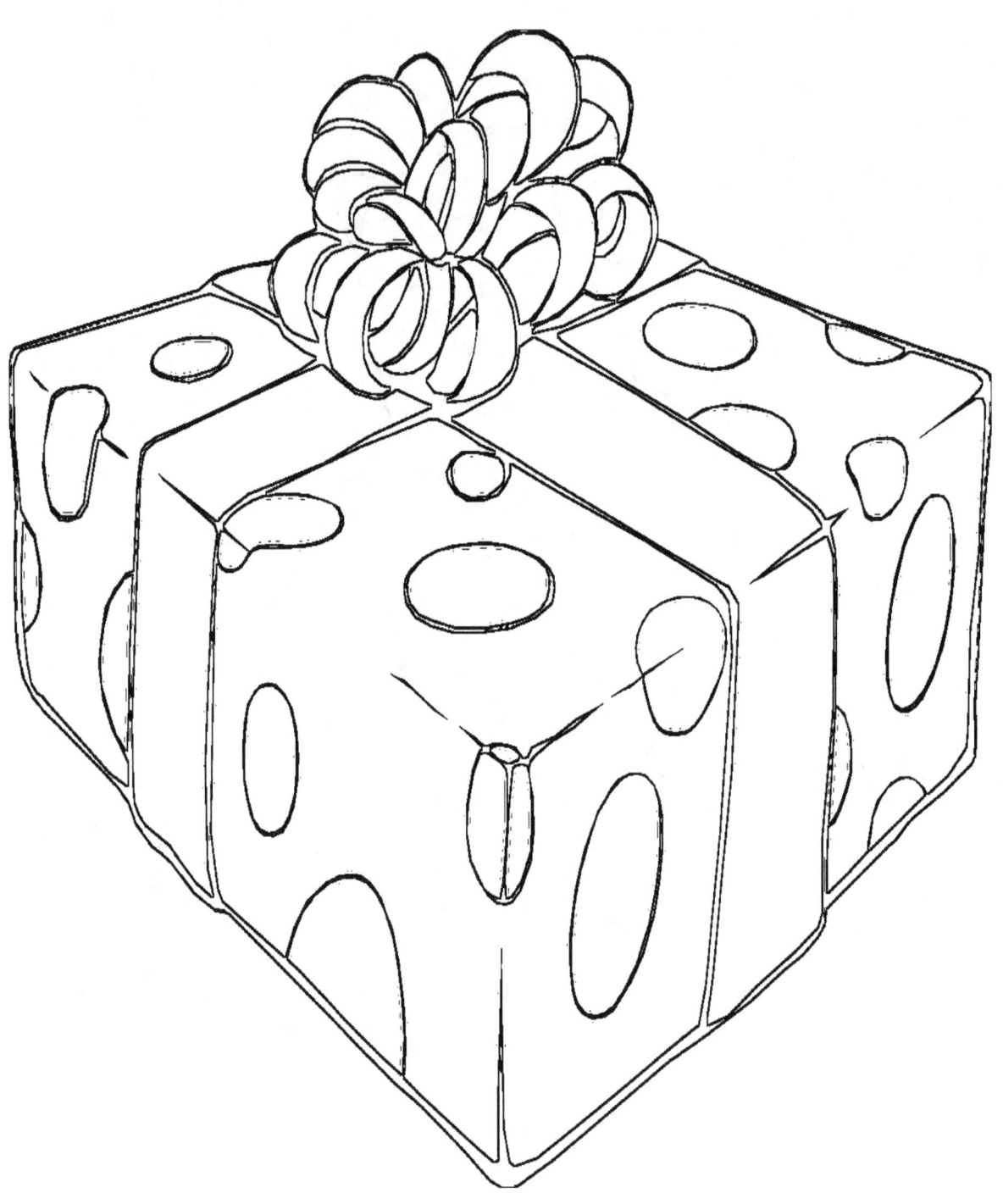

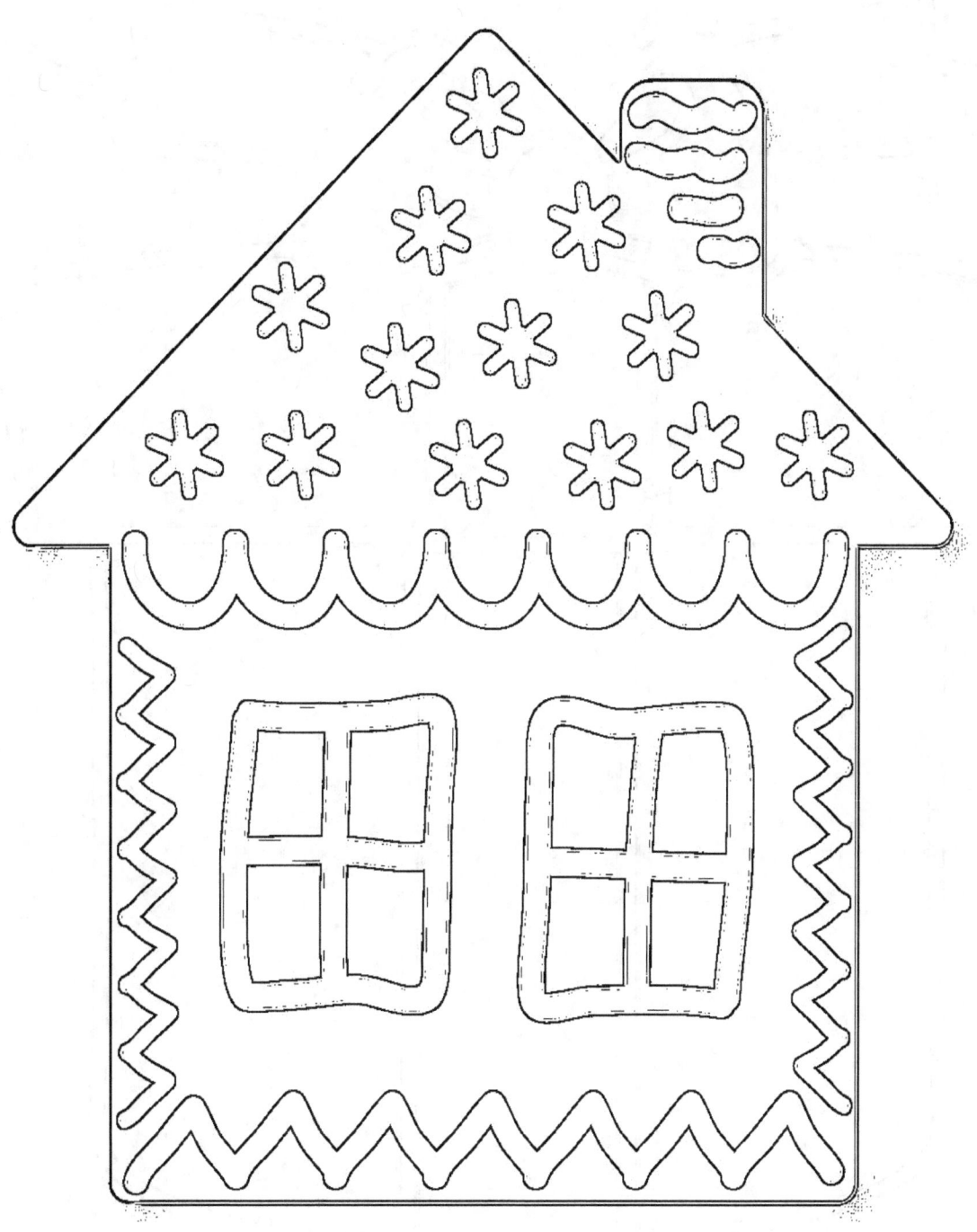

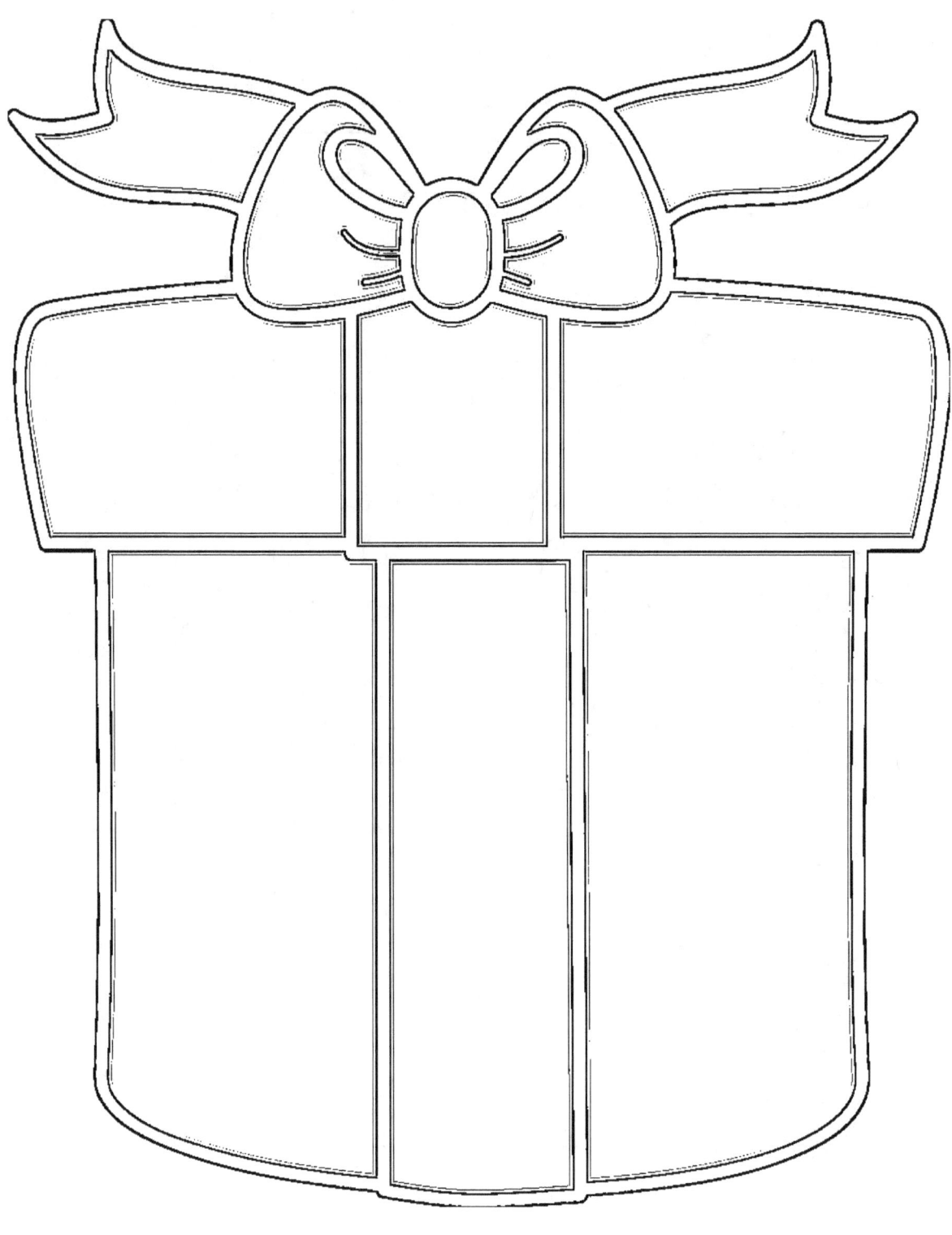

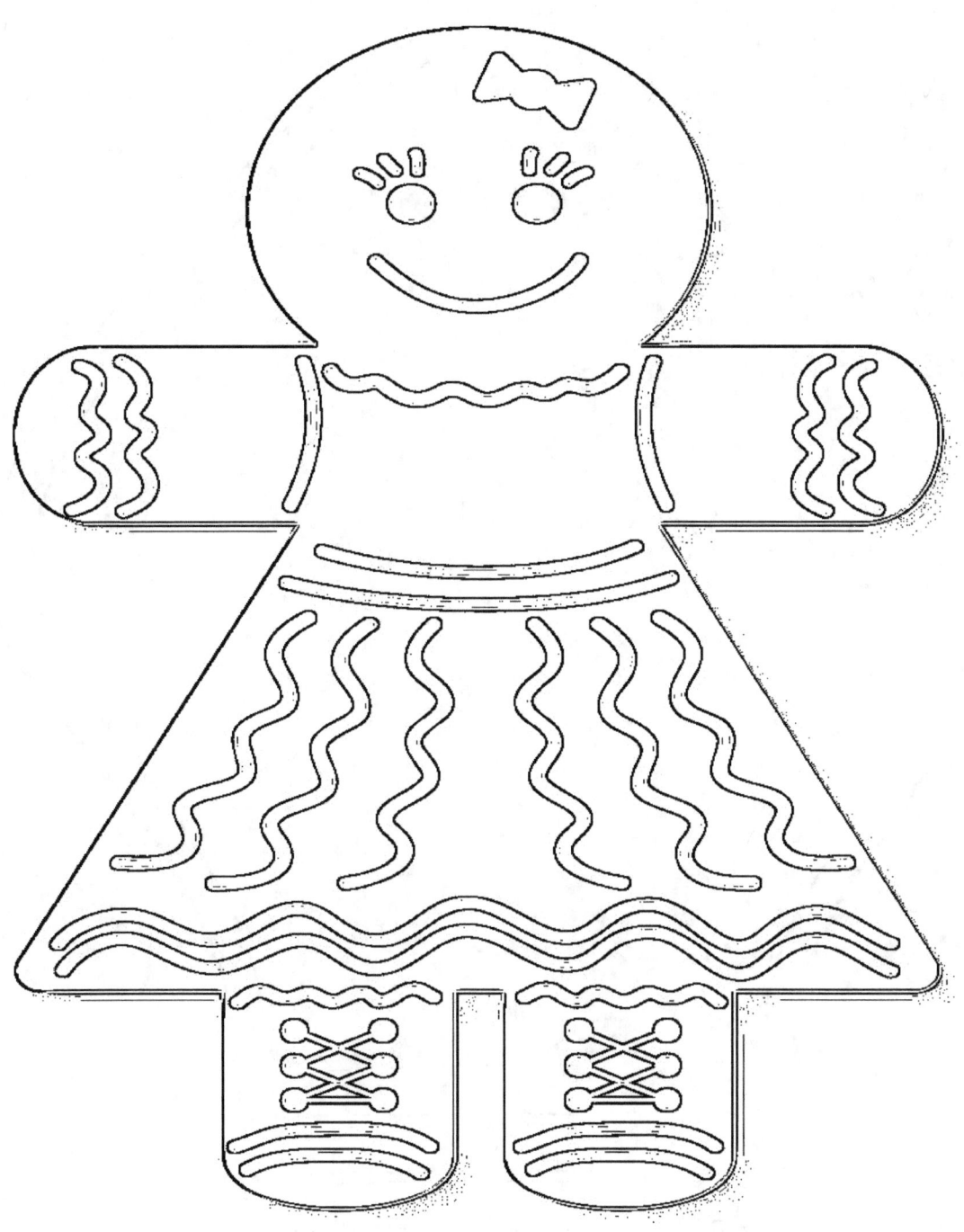

Peace On Earth, A King Is Born

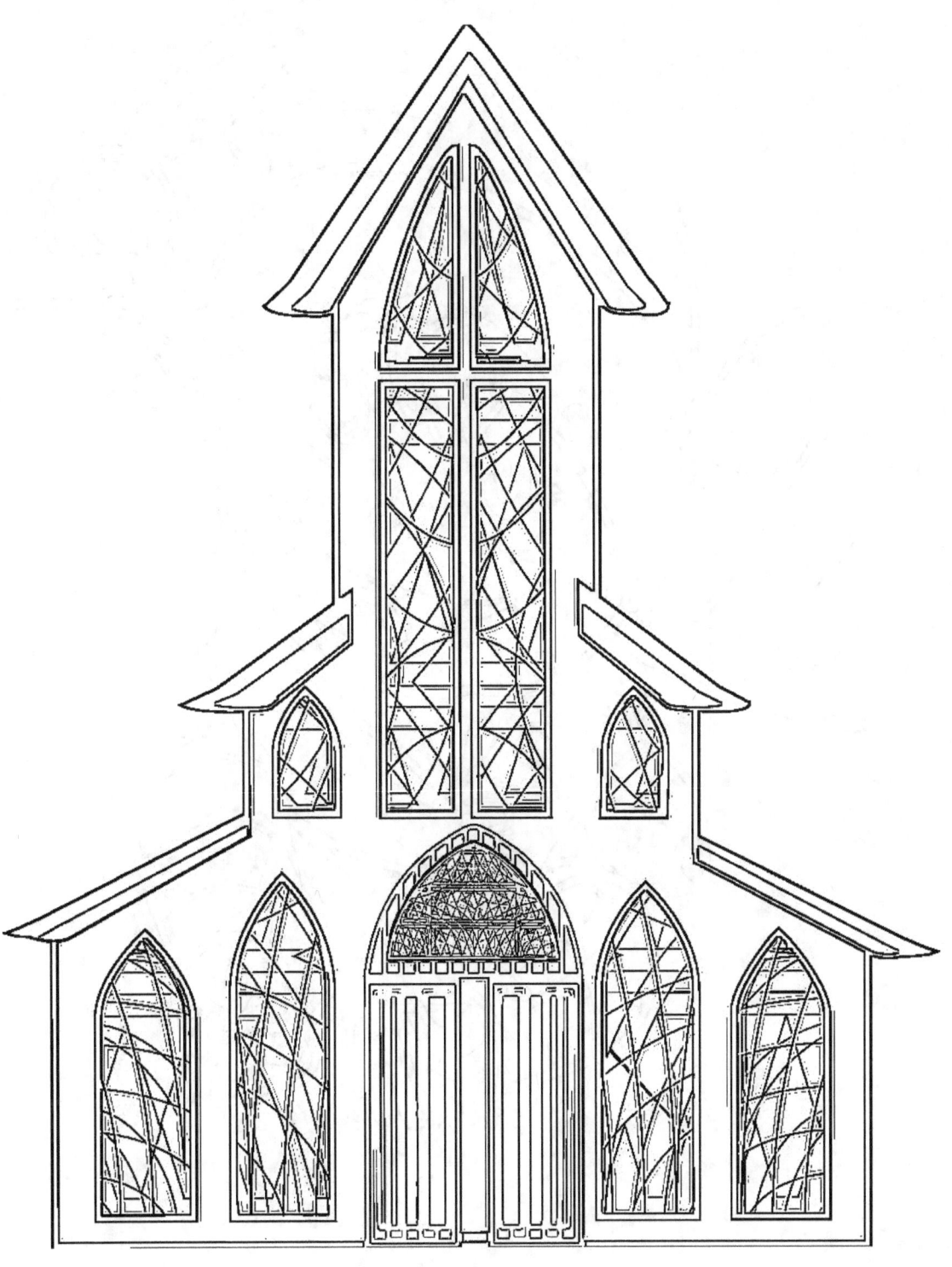

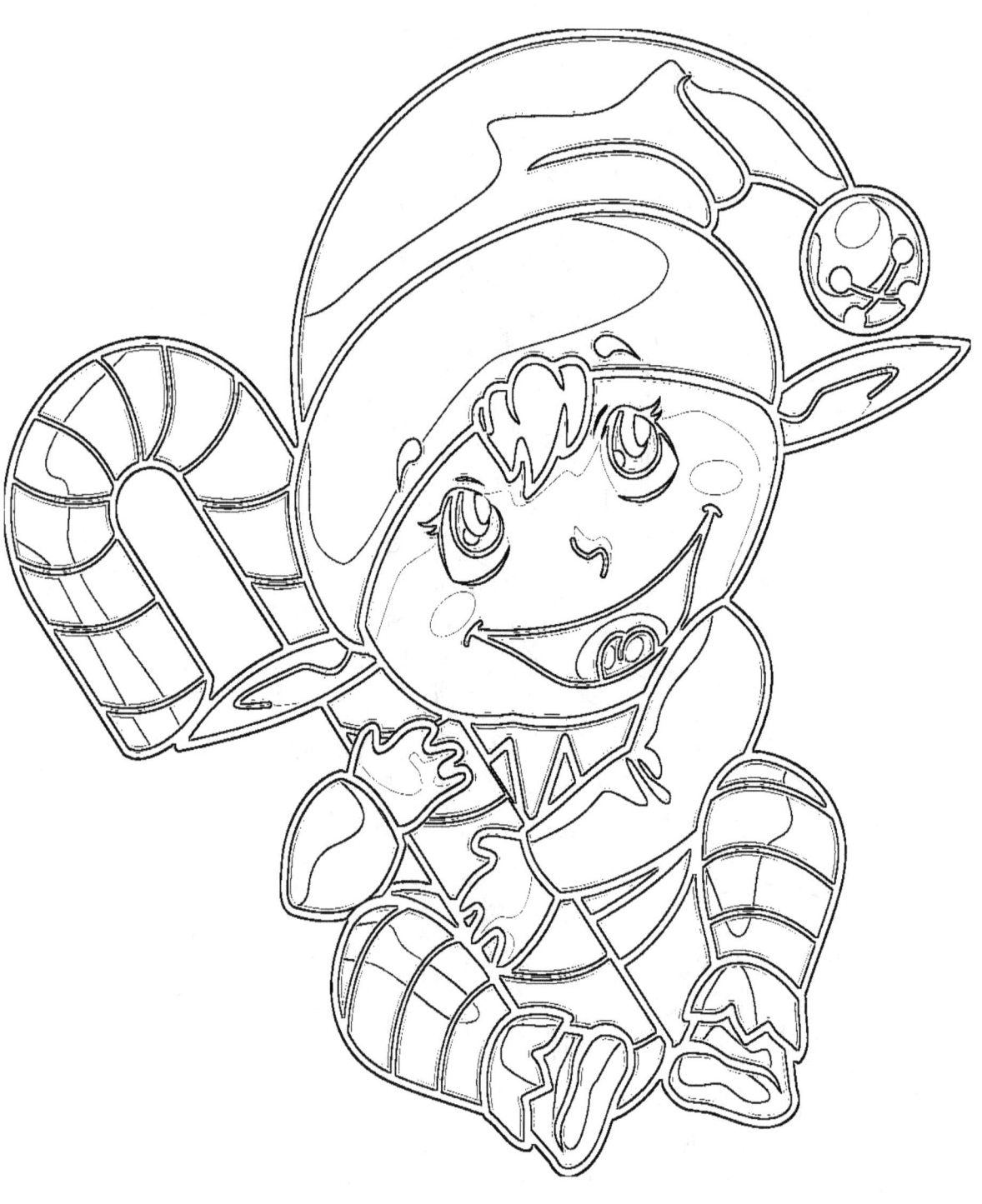

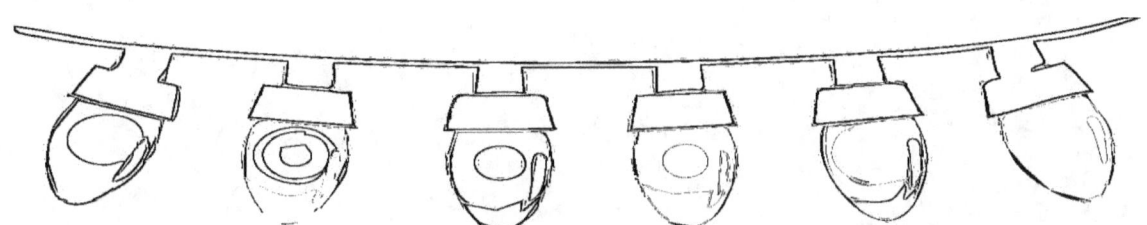

MERRY CHRISTMAS
AND
HAPPPY NEW YEAR

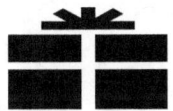

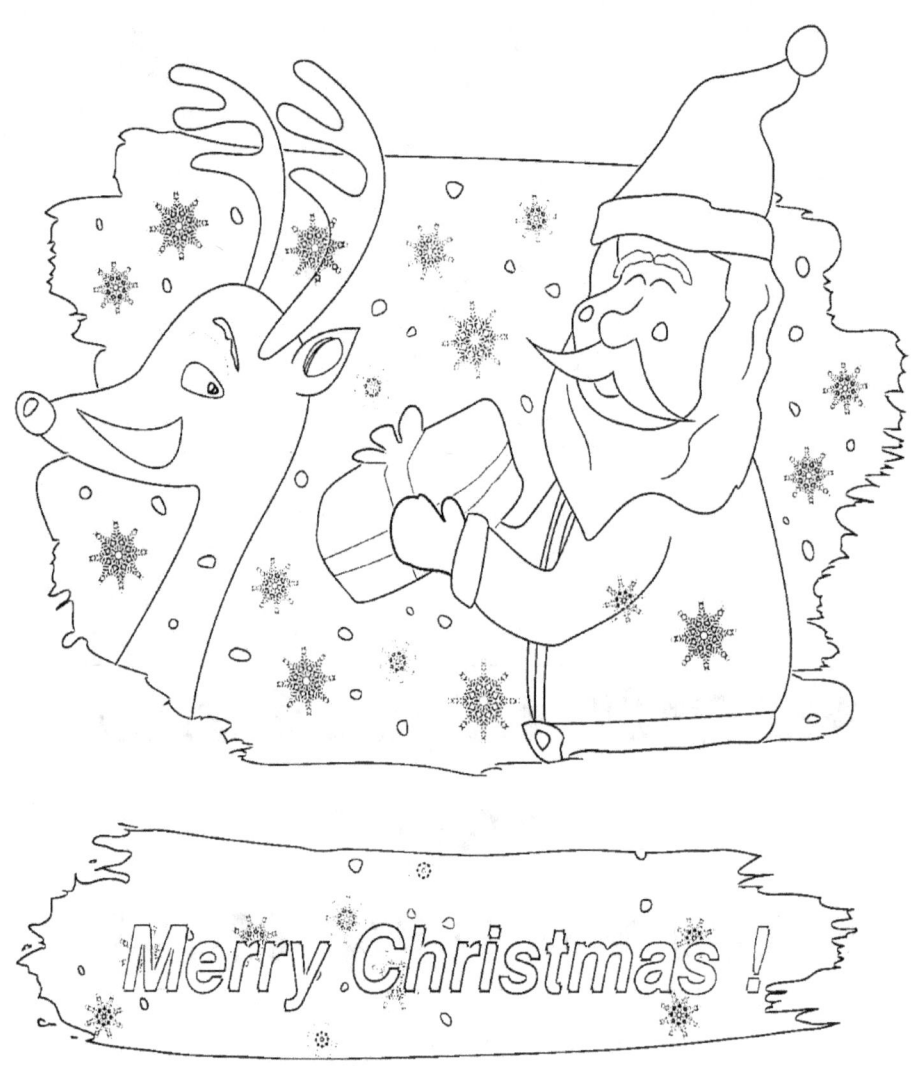

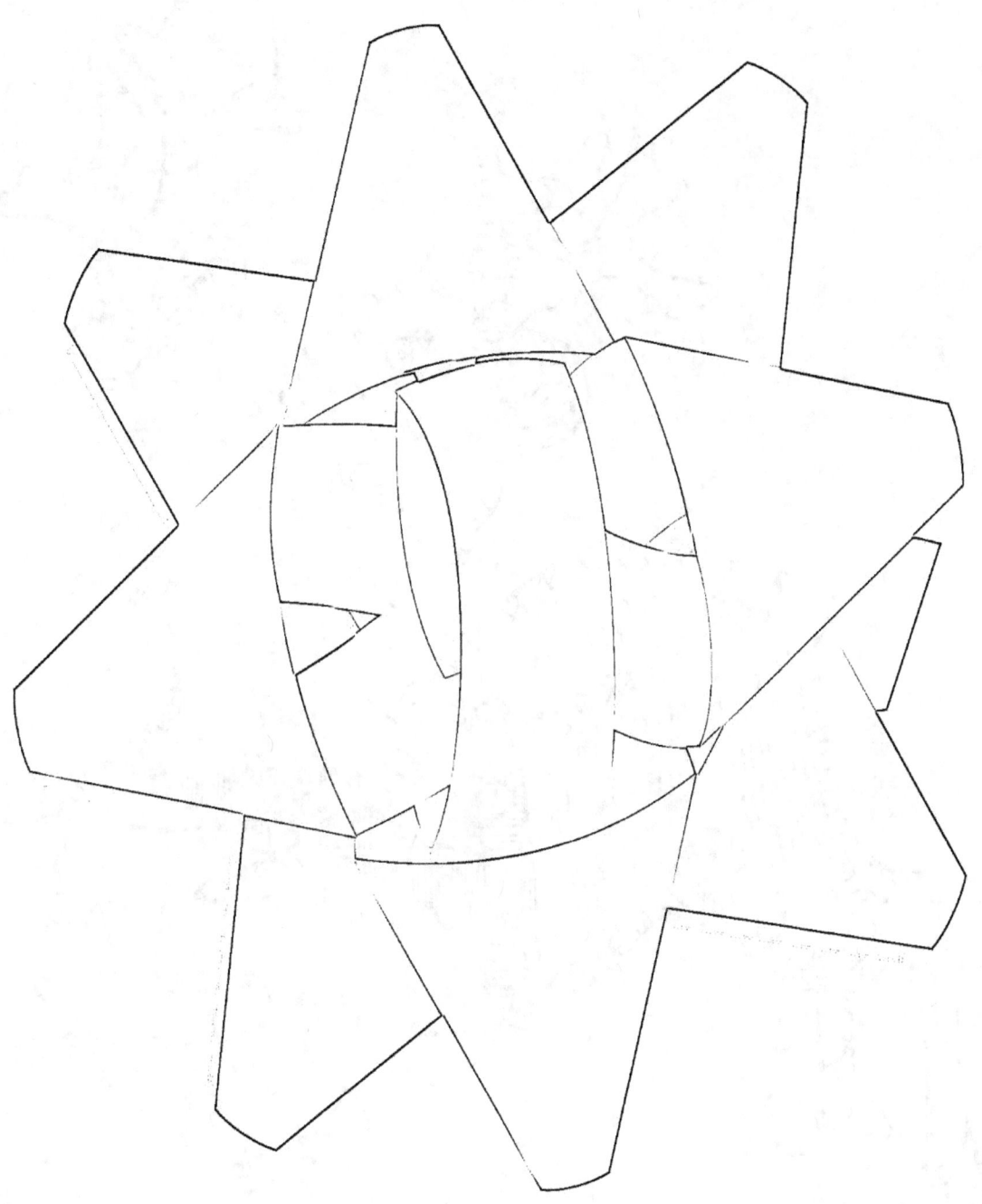

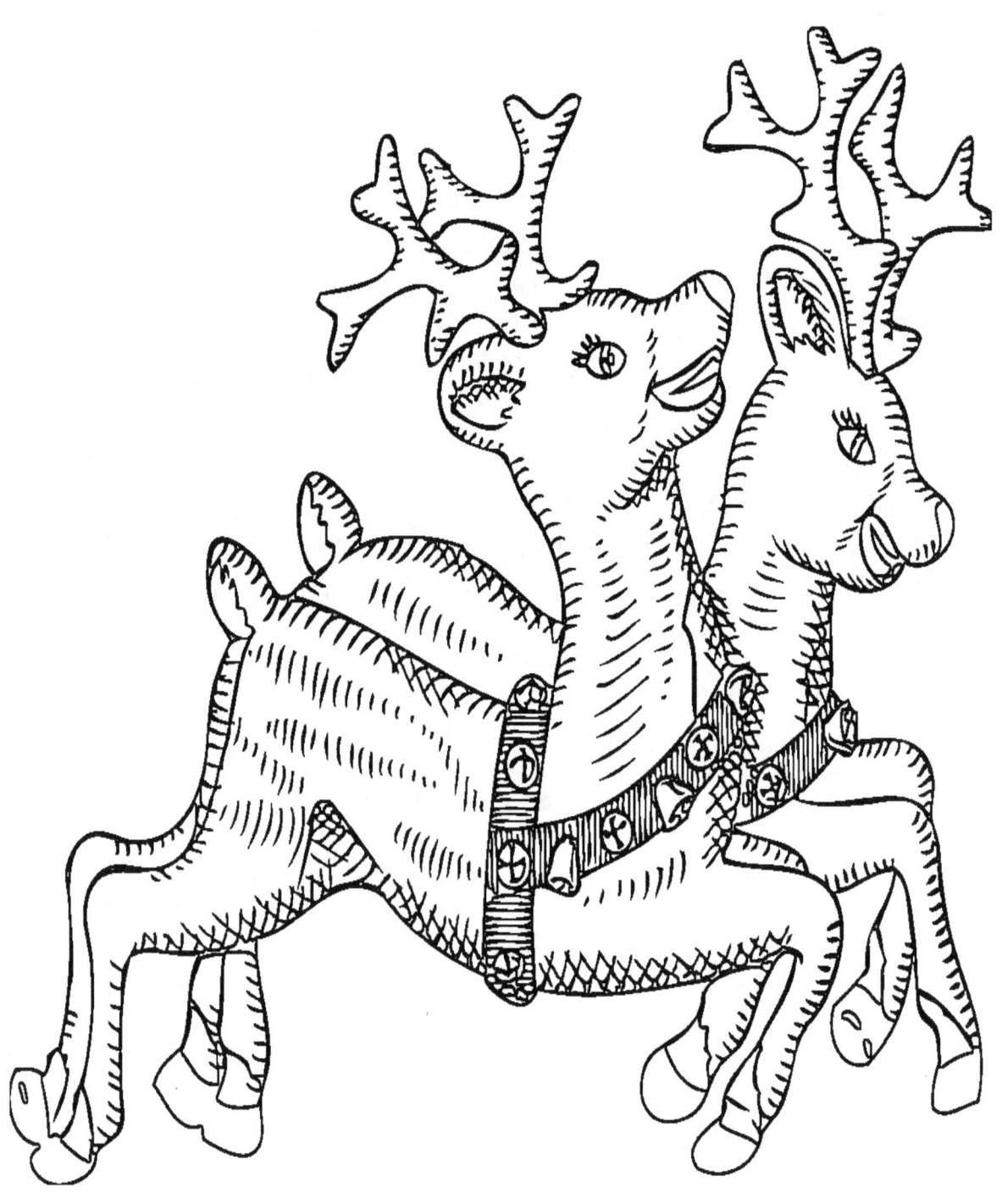

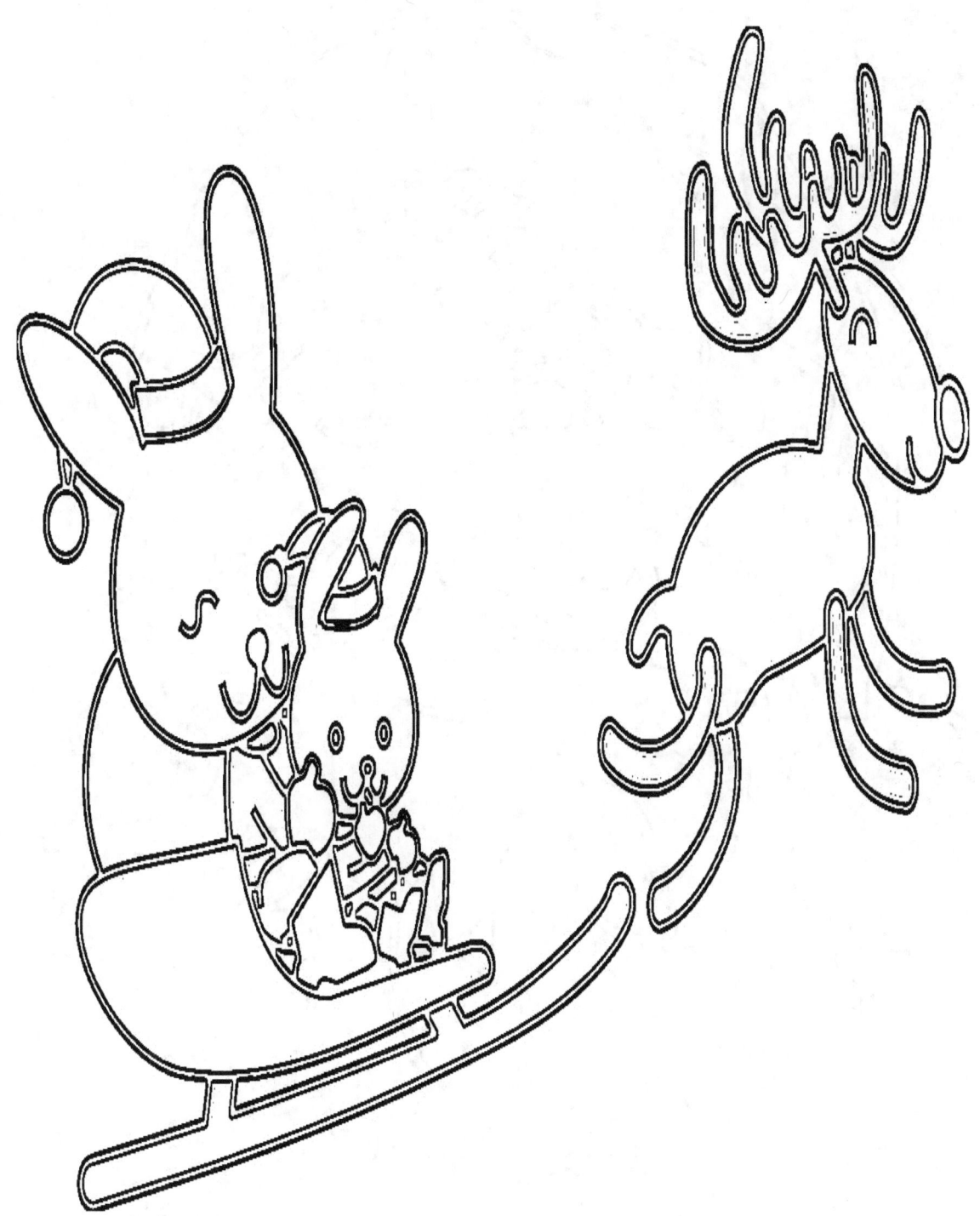

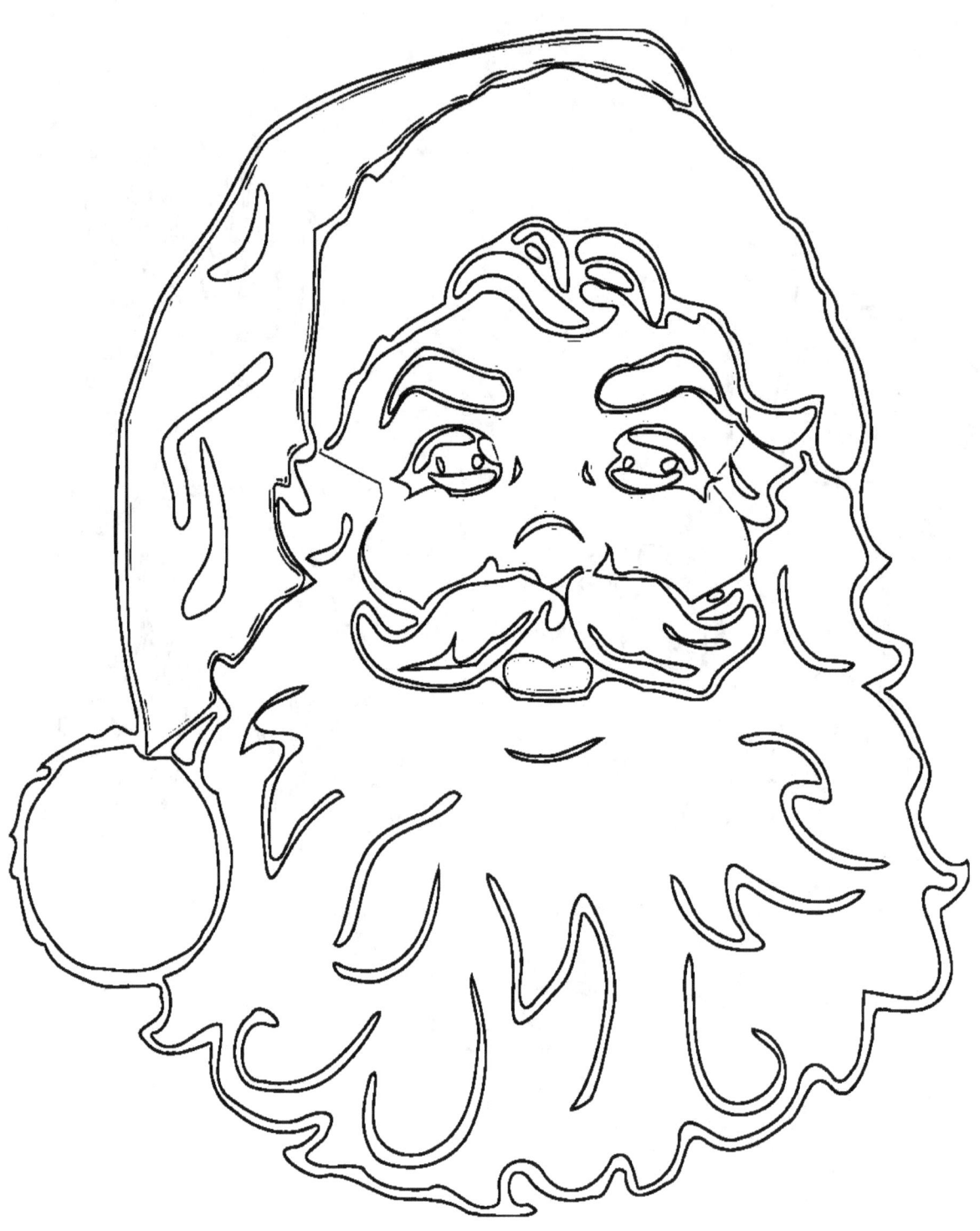

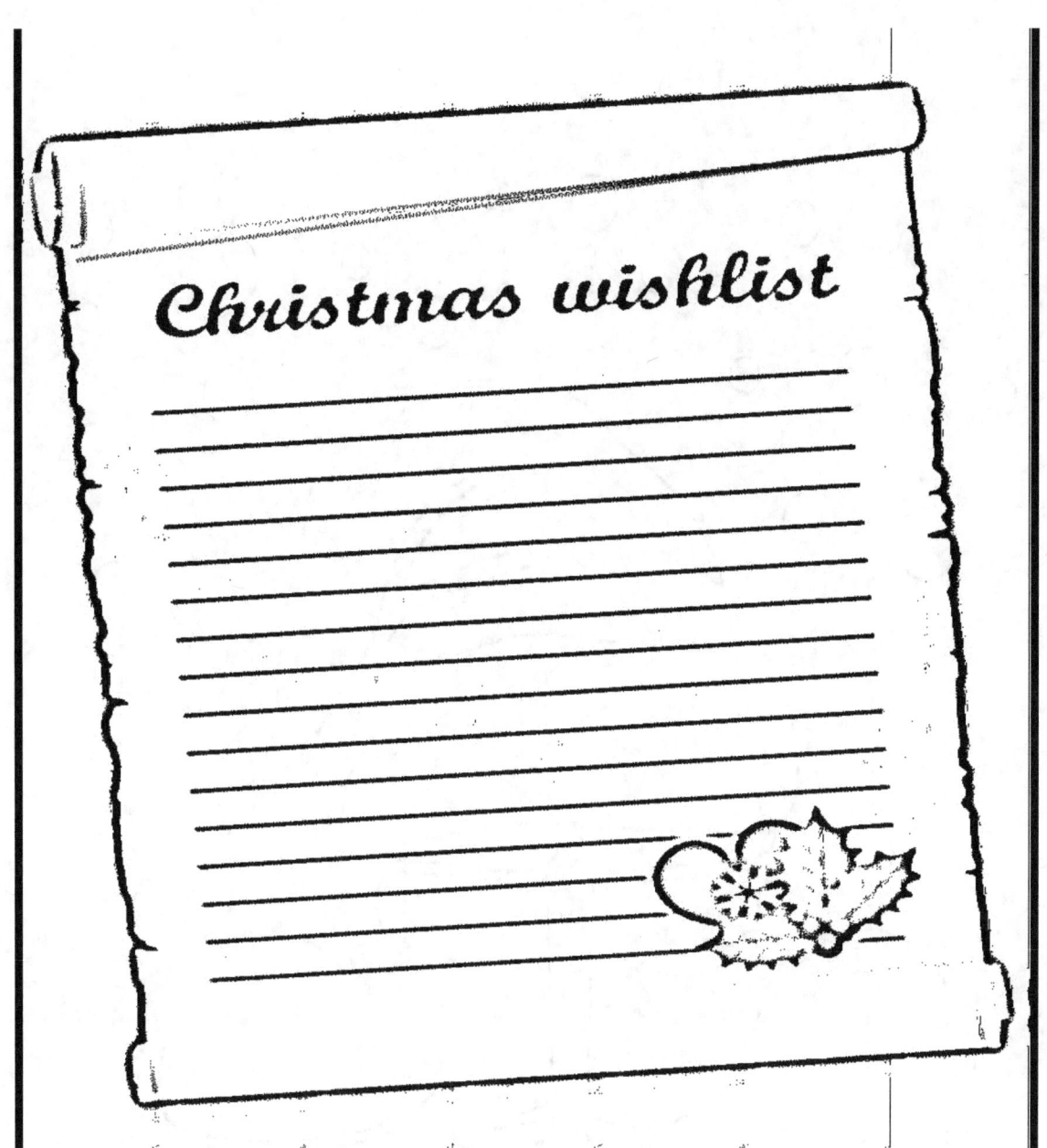

My Family's Wish List To Santa:

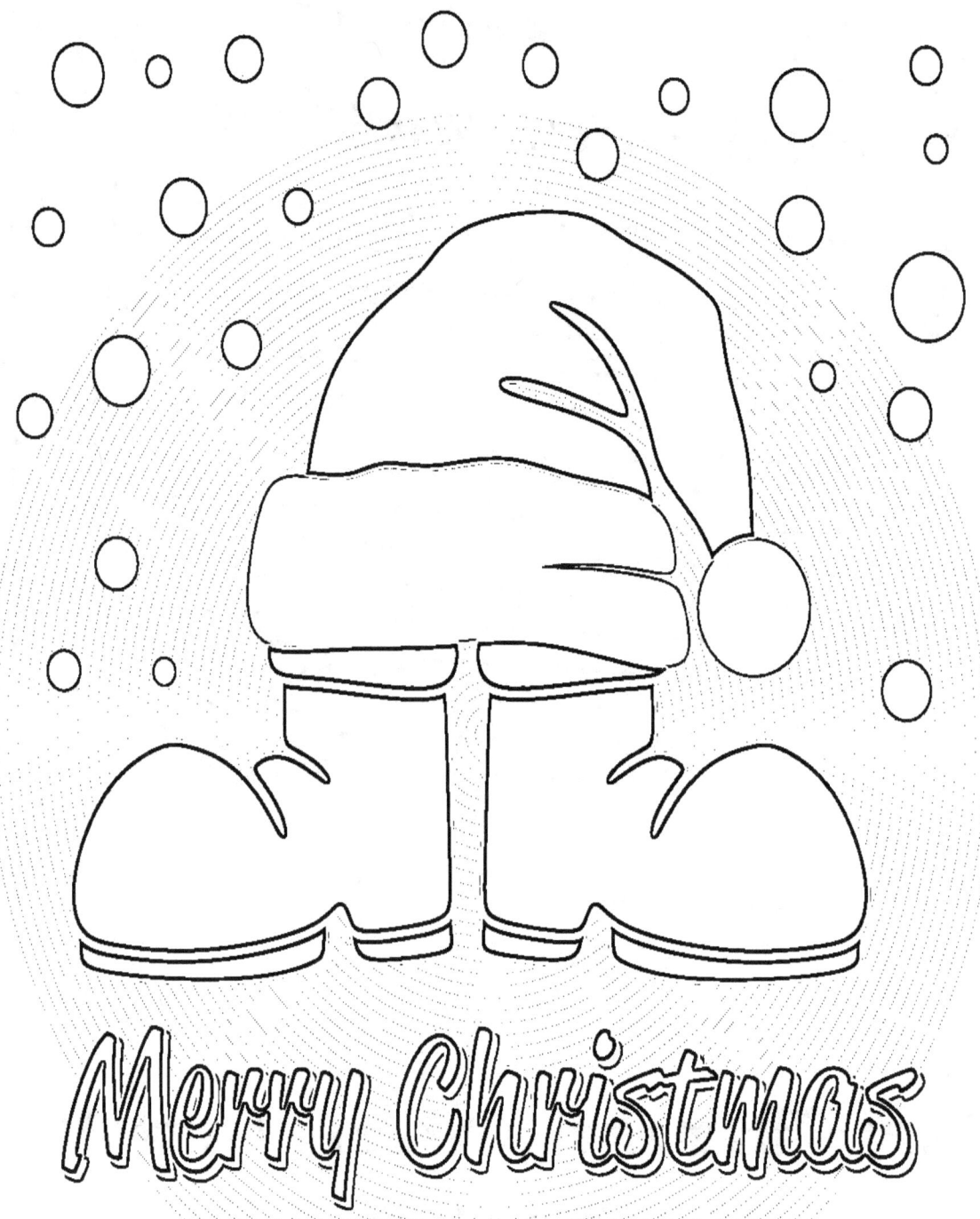

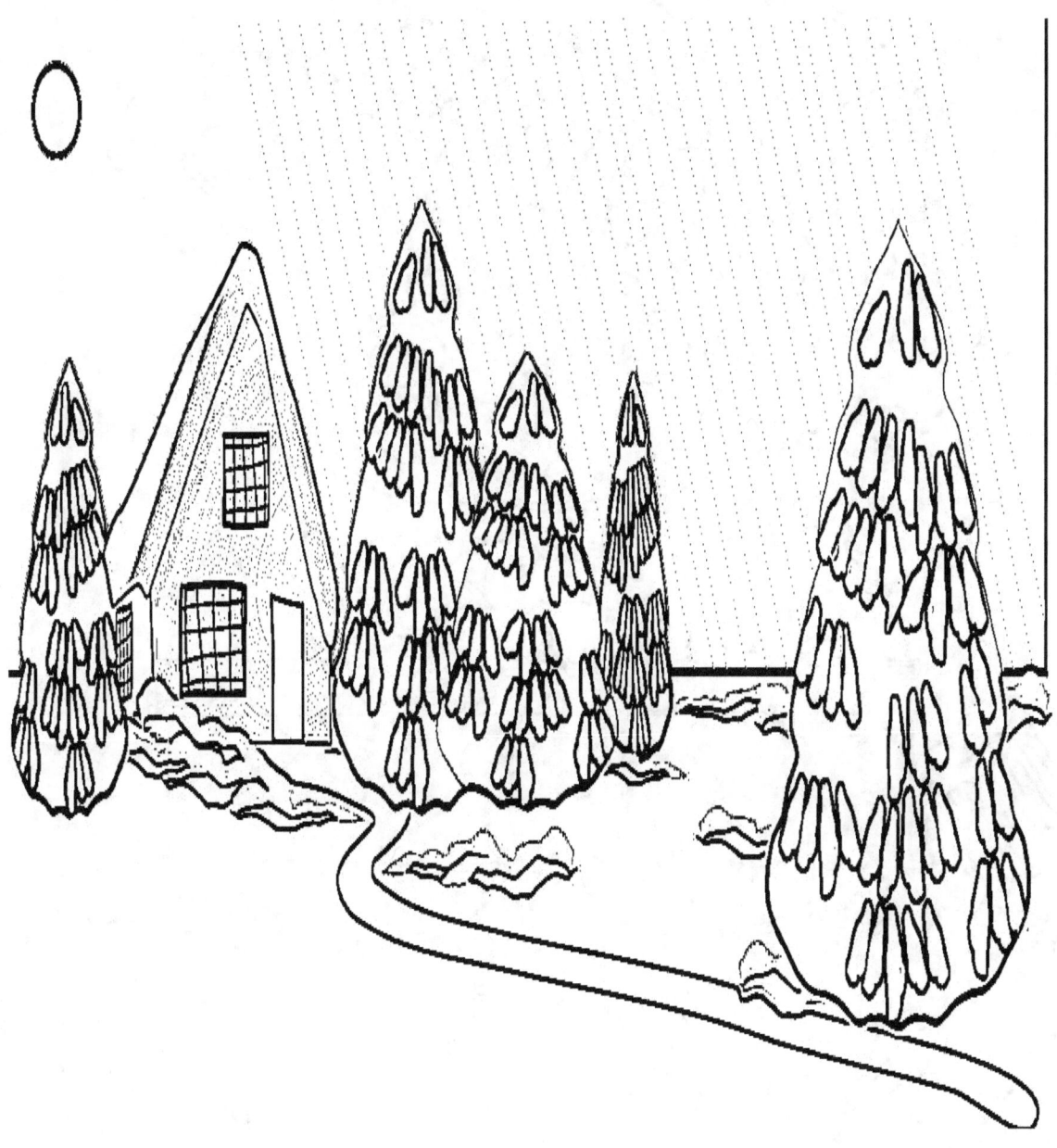

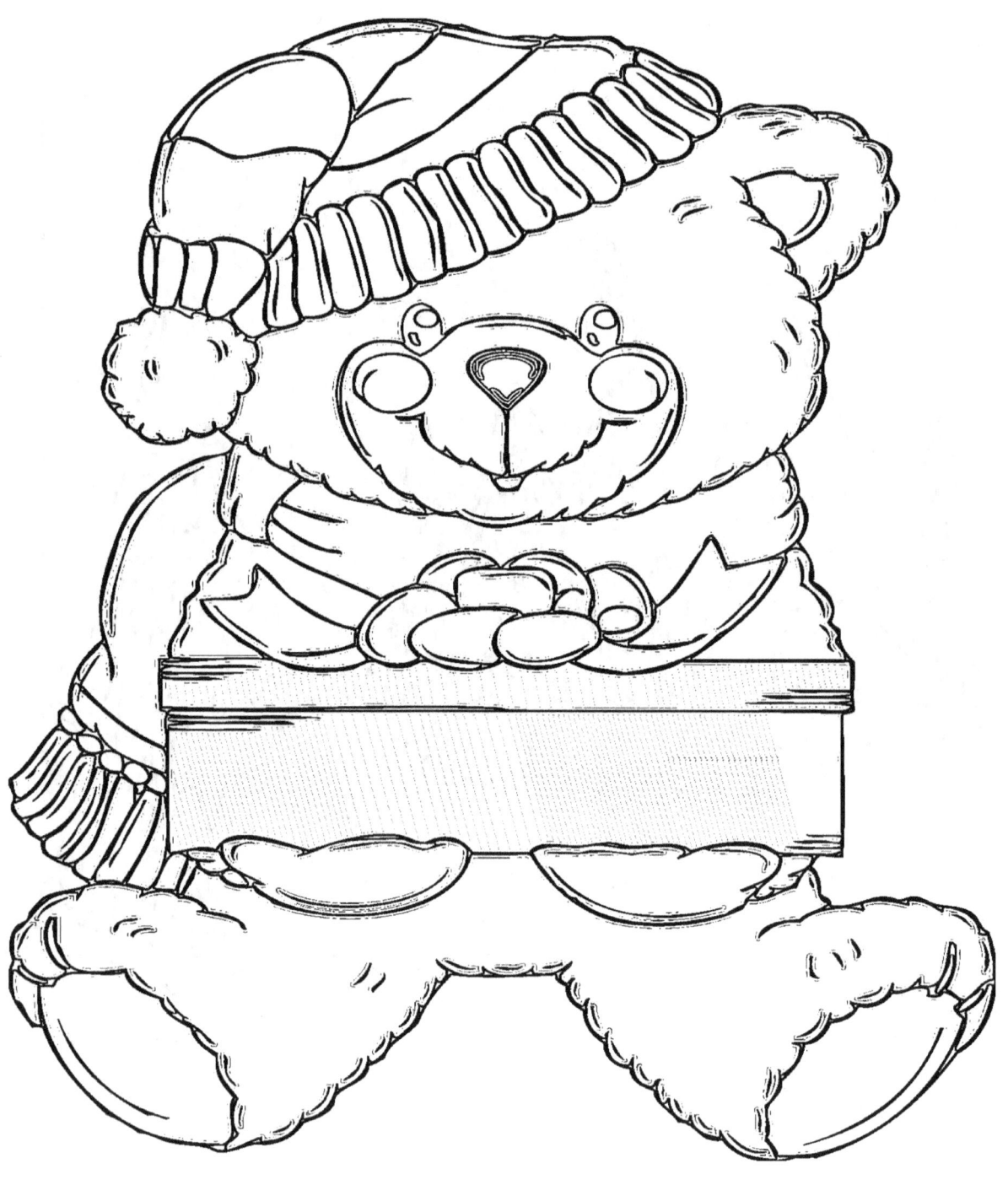

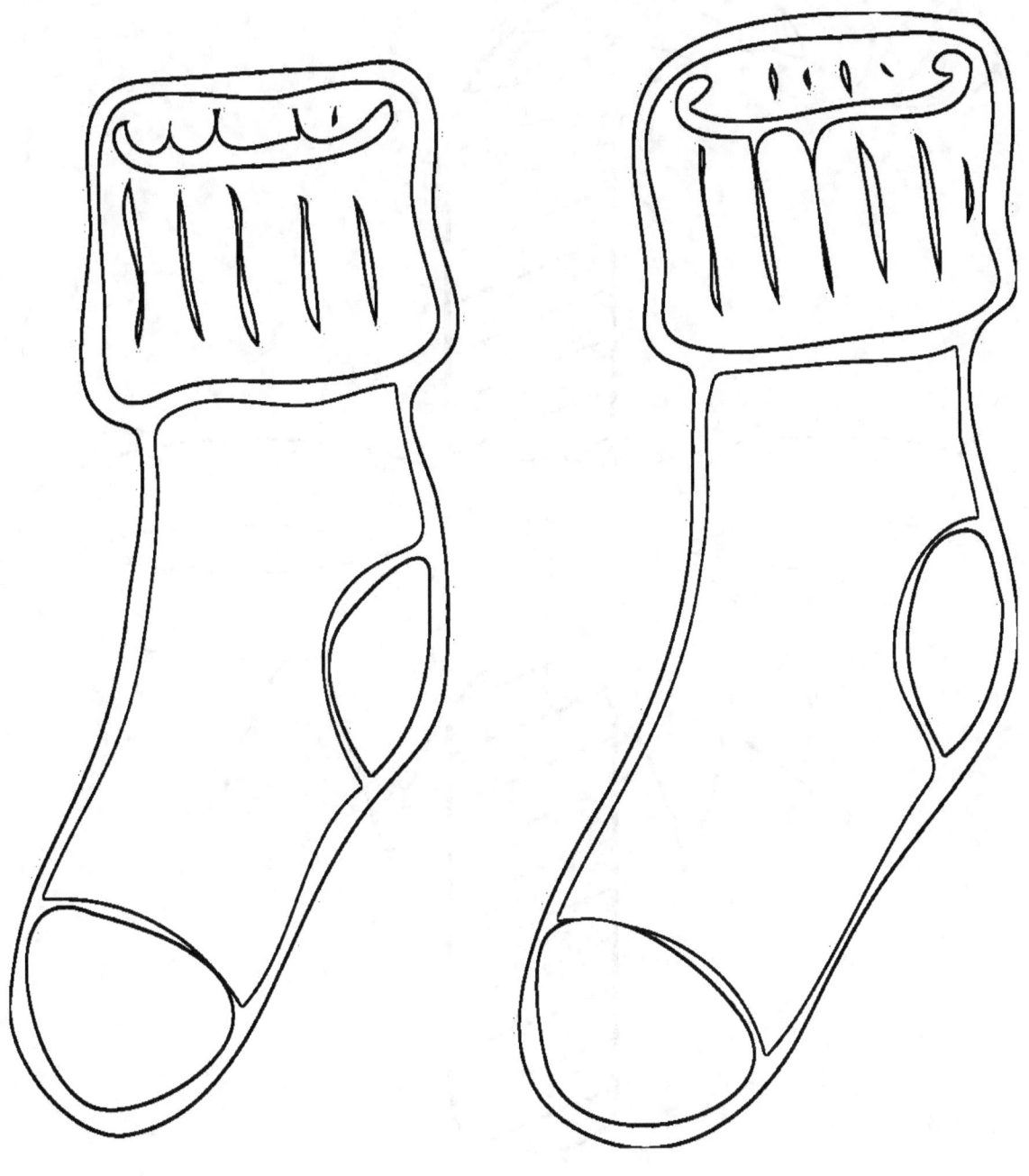

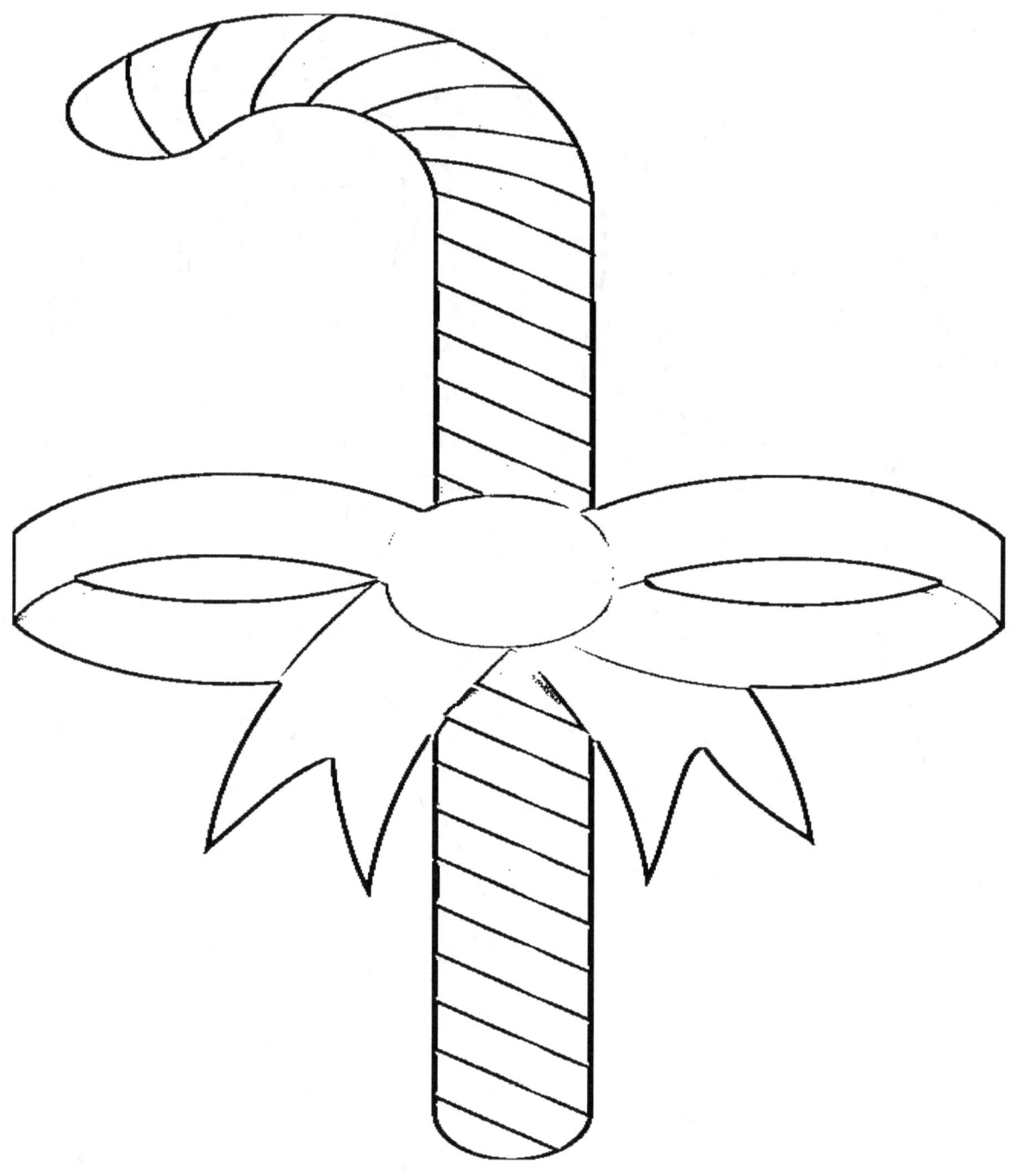

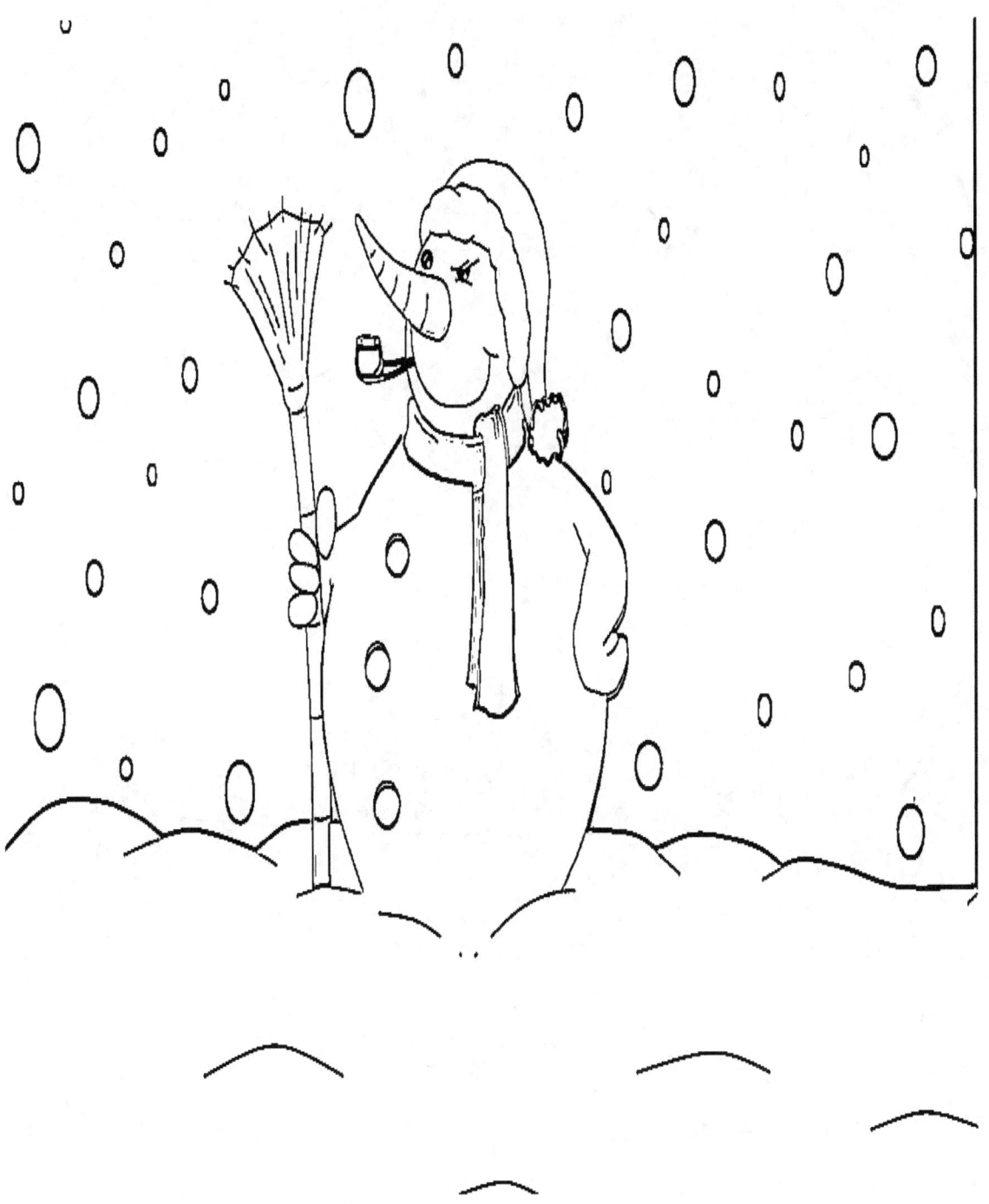

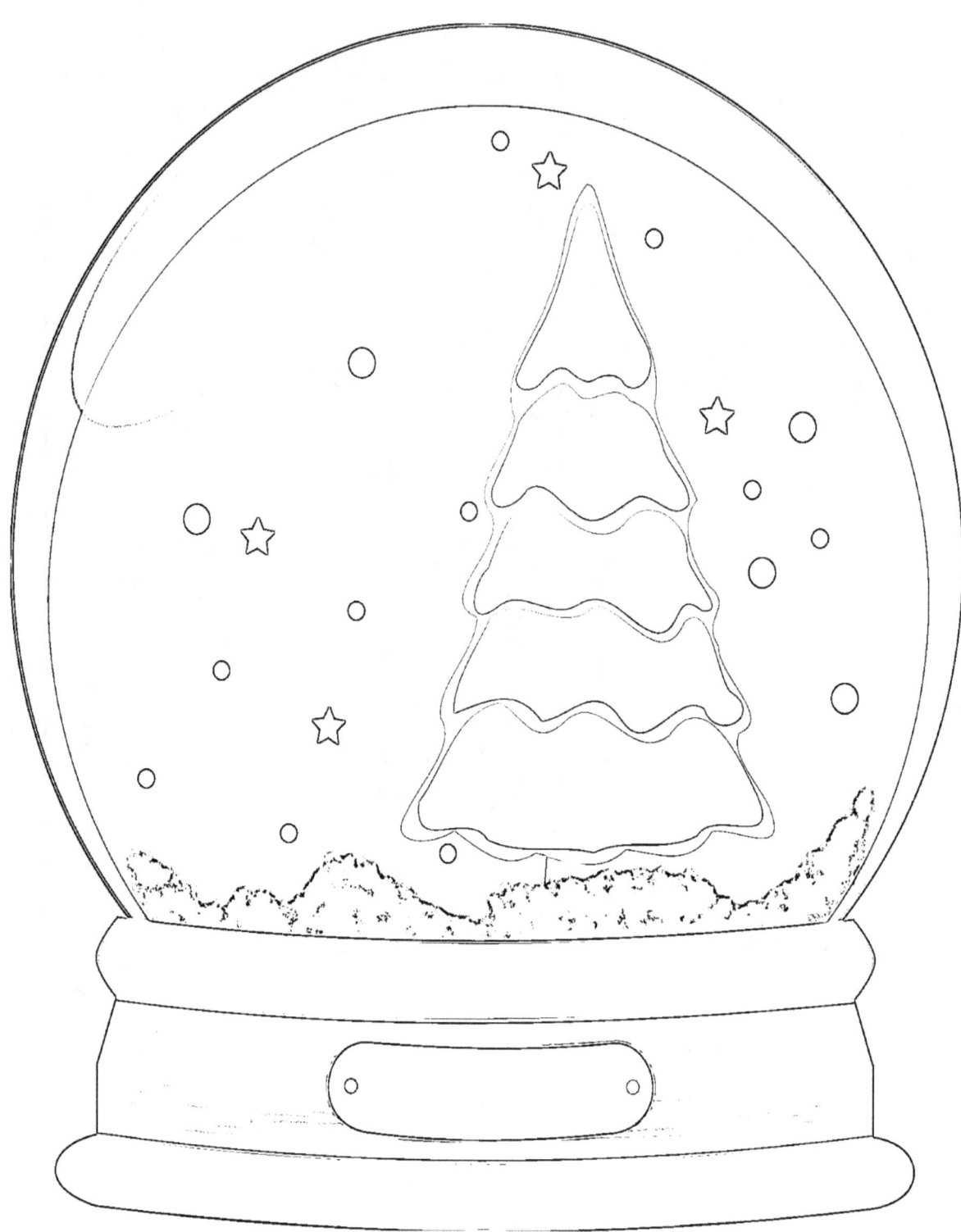

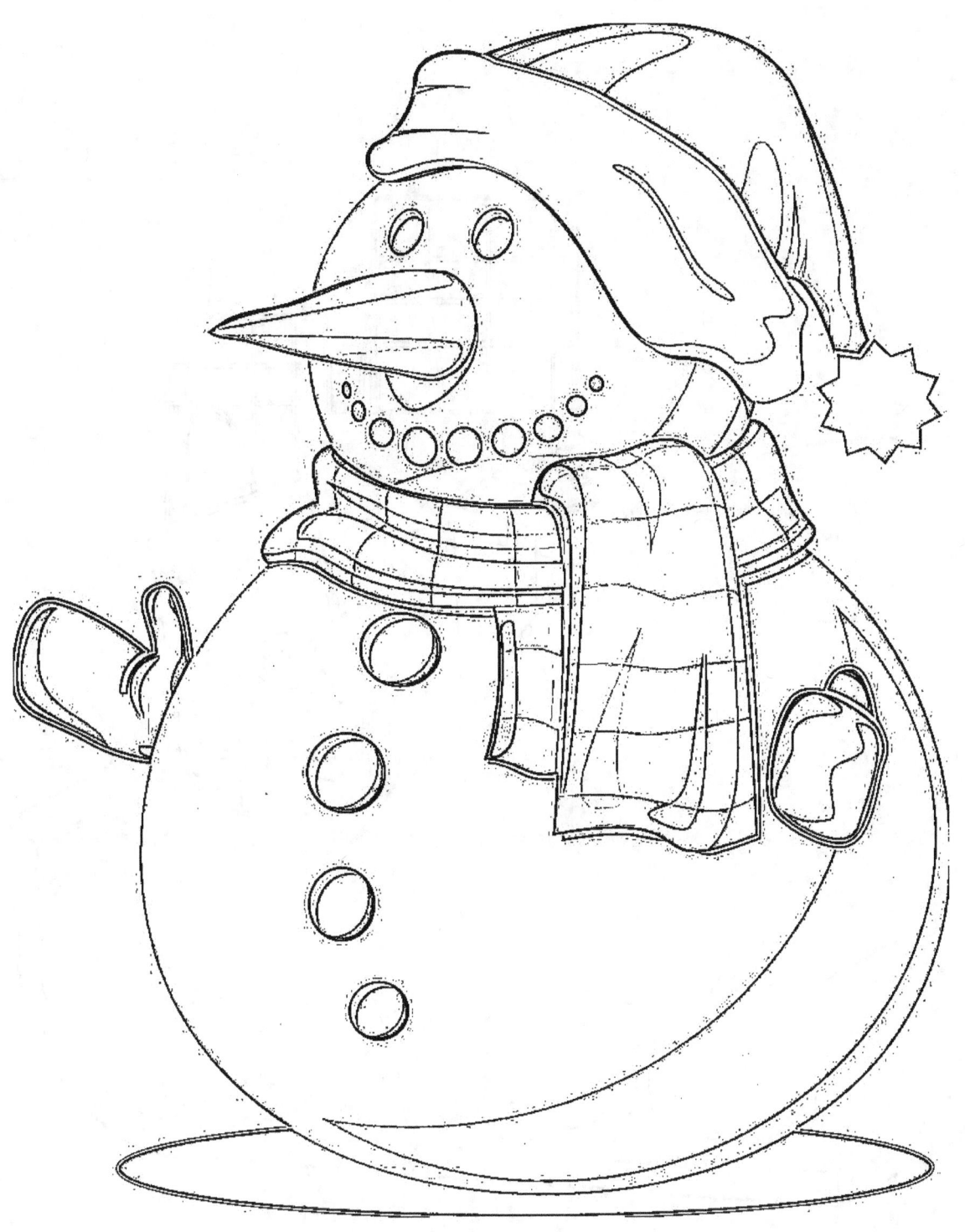

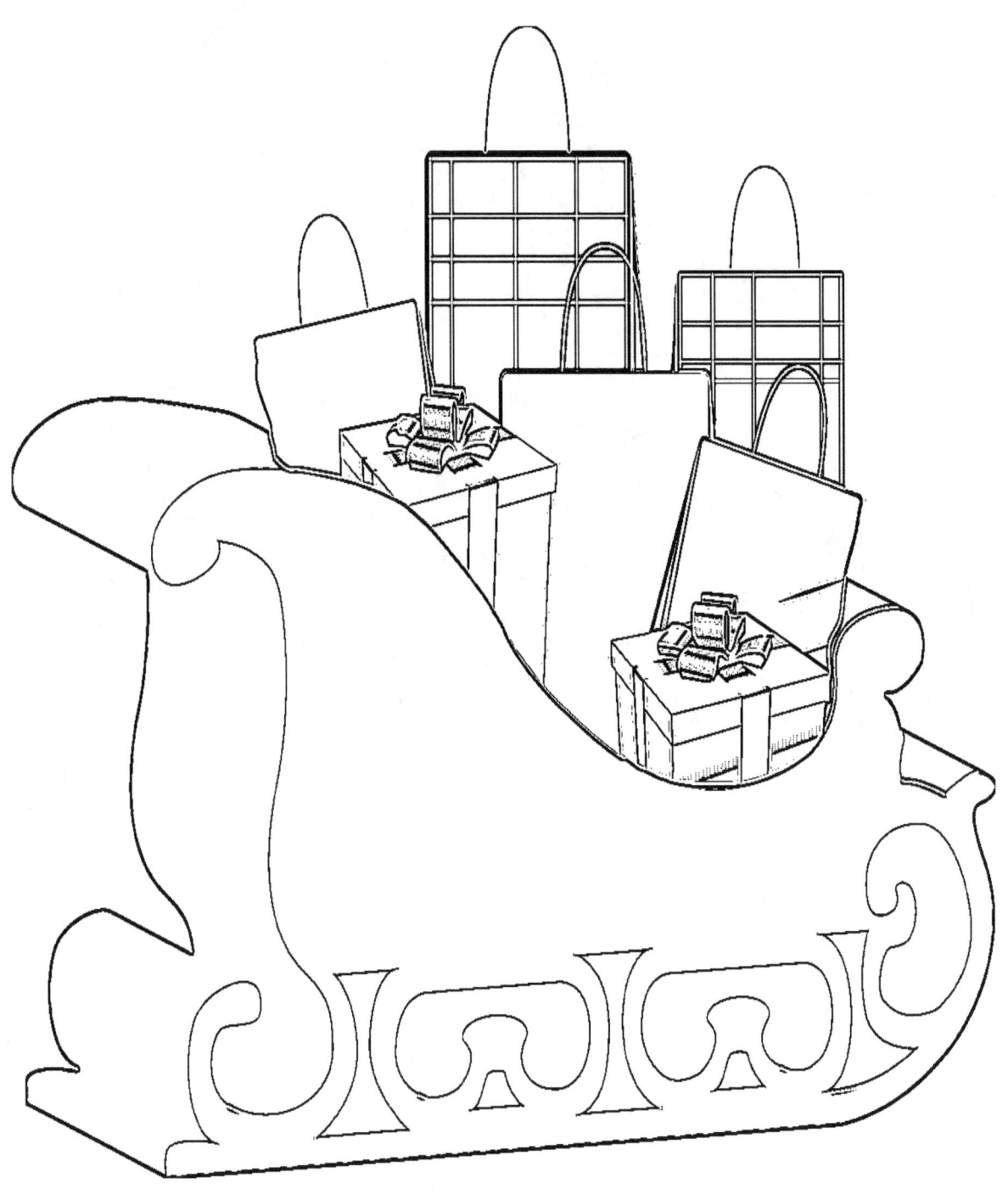

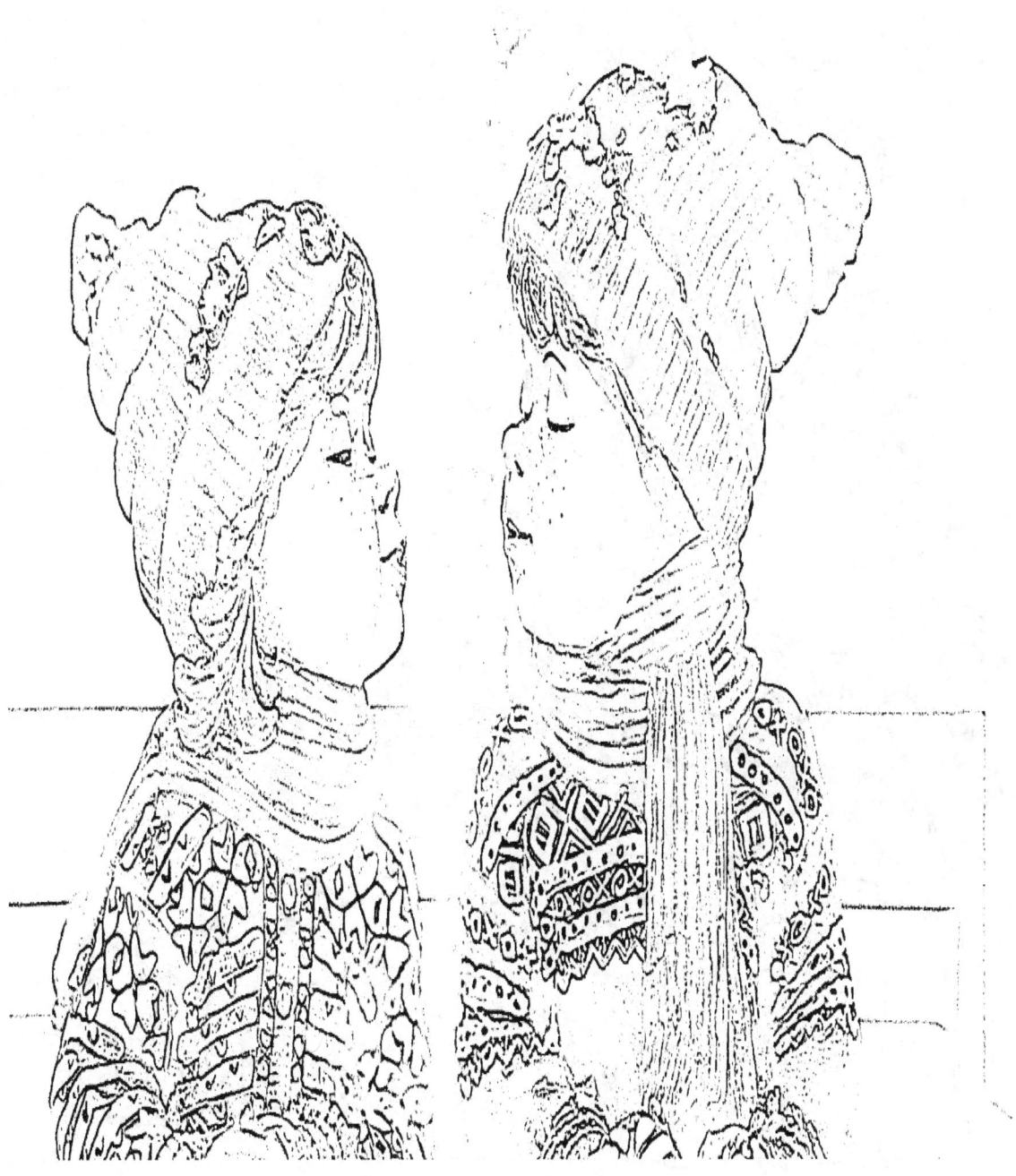

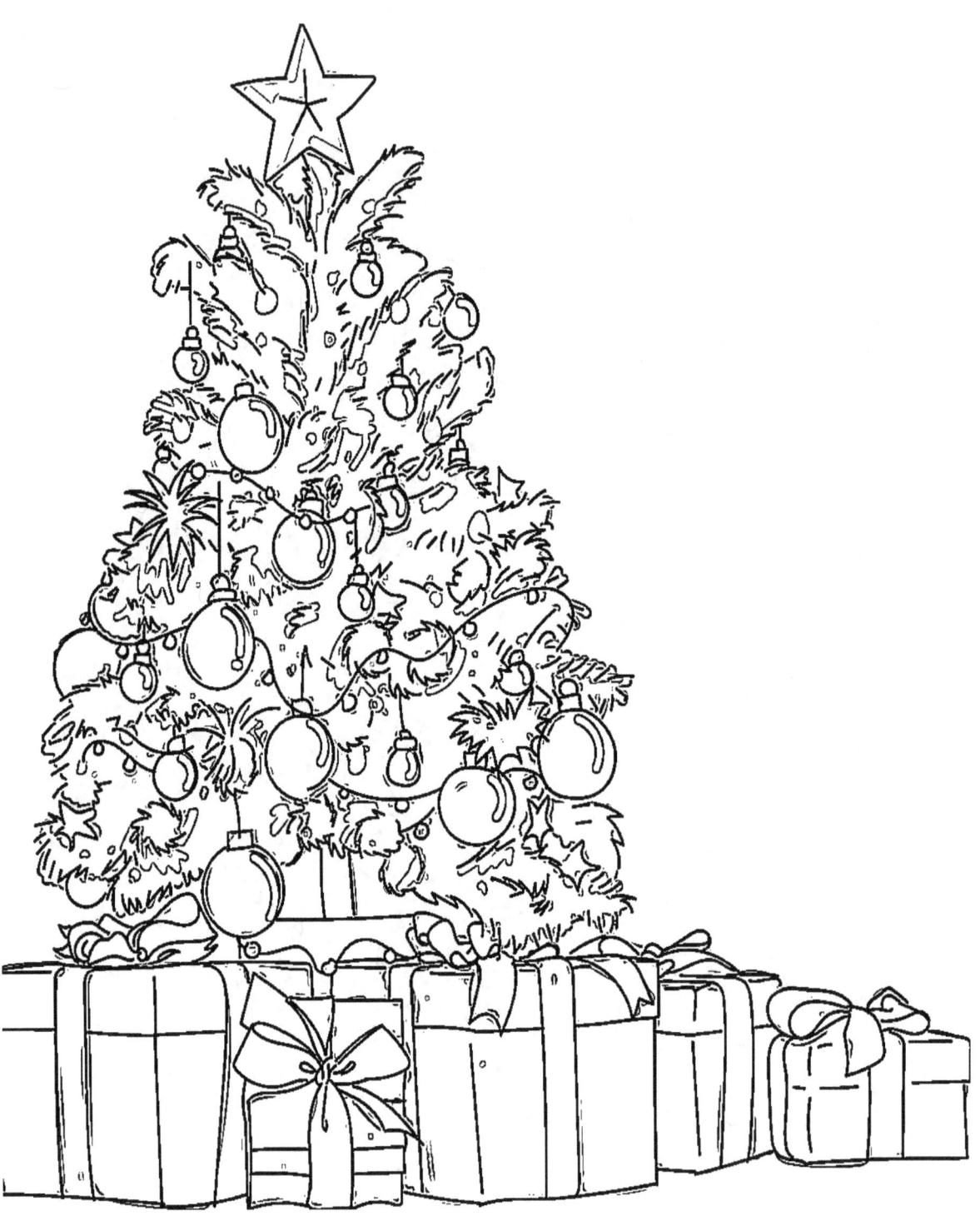

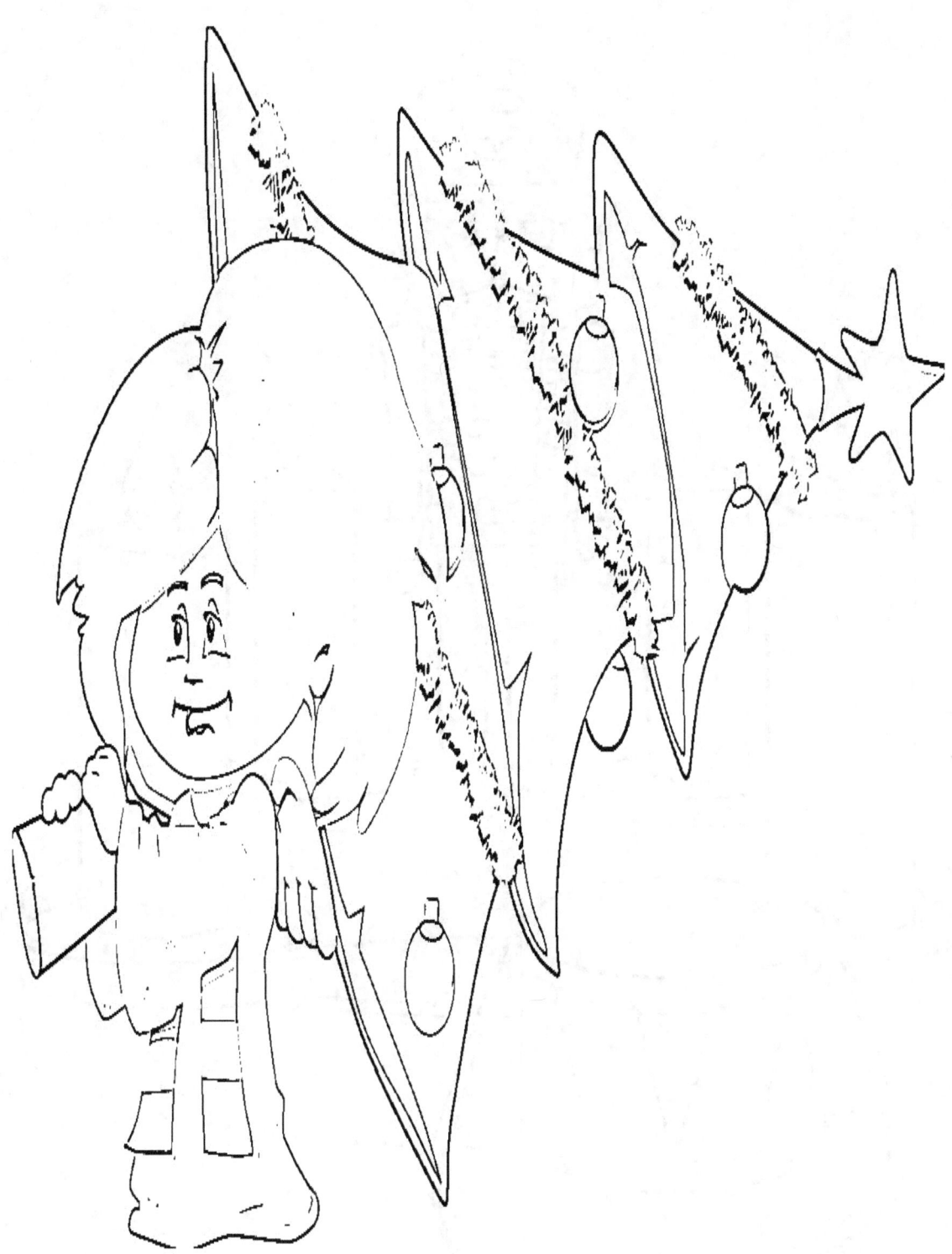

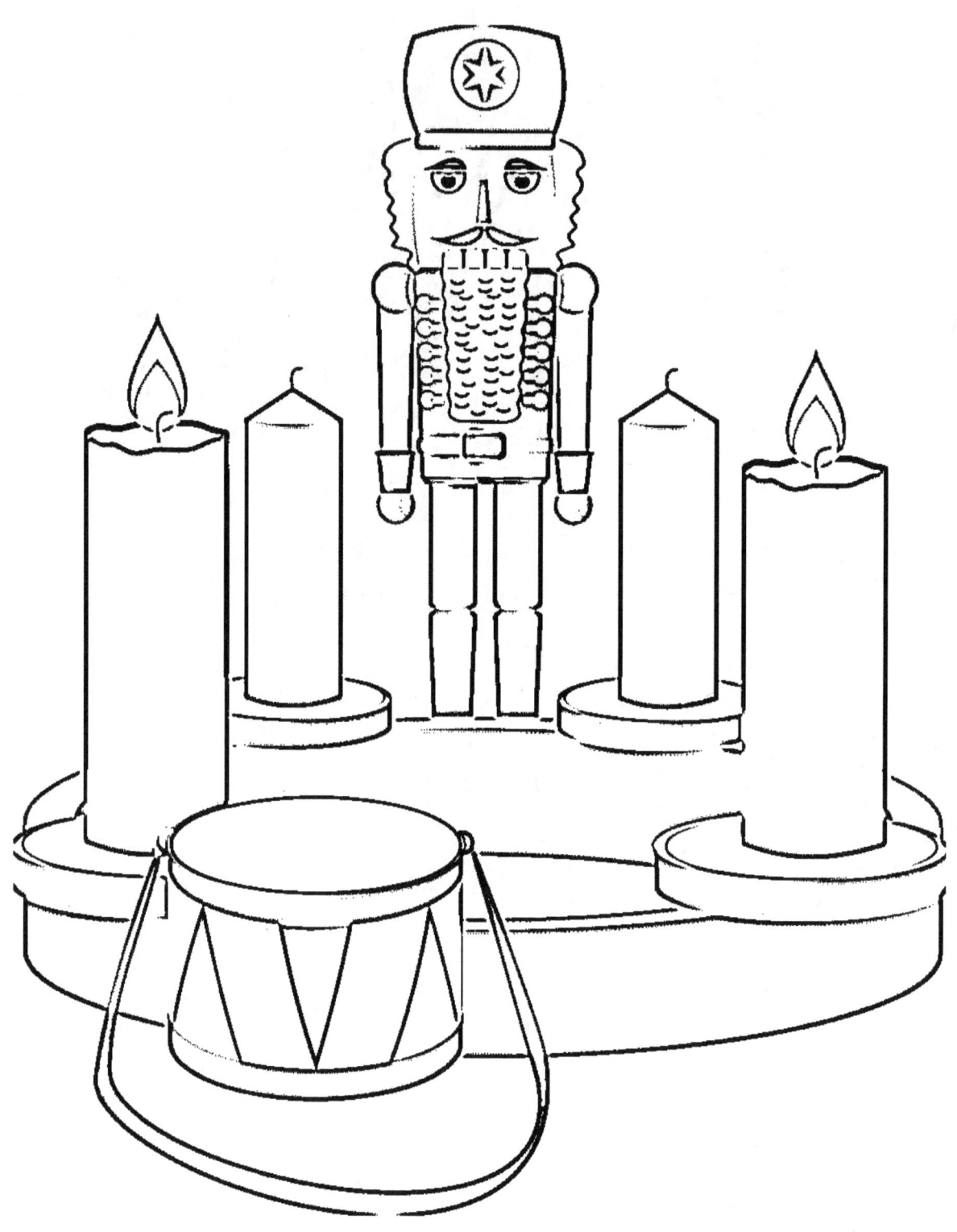

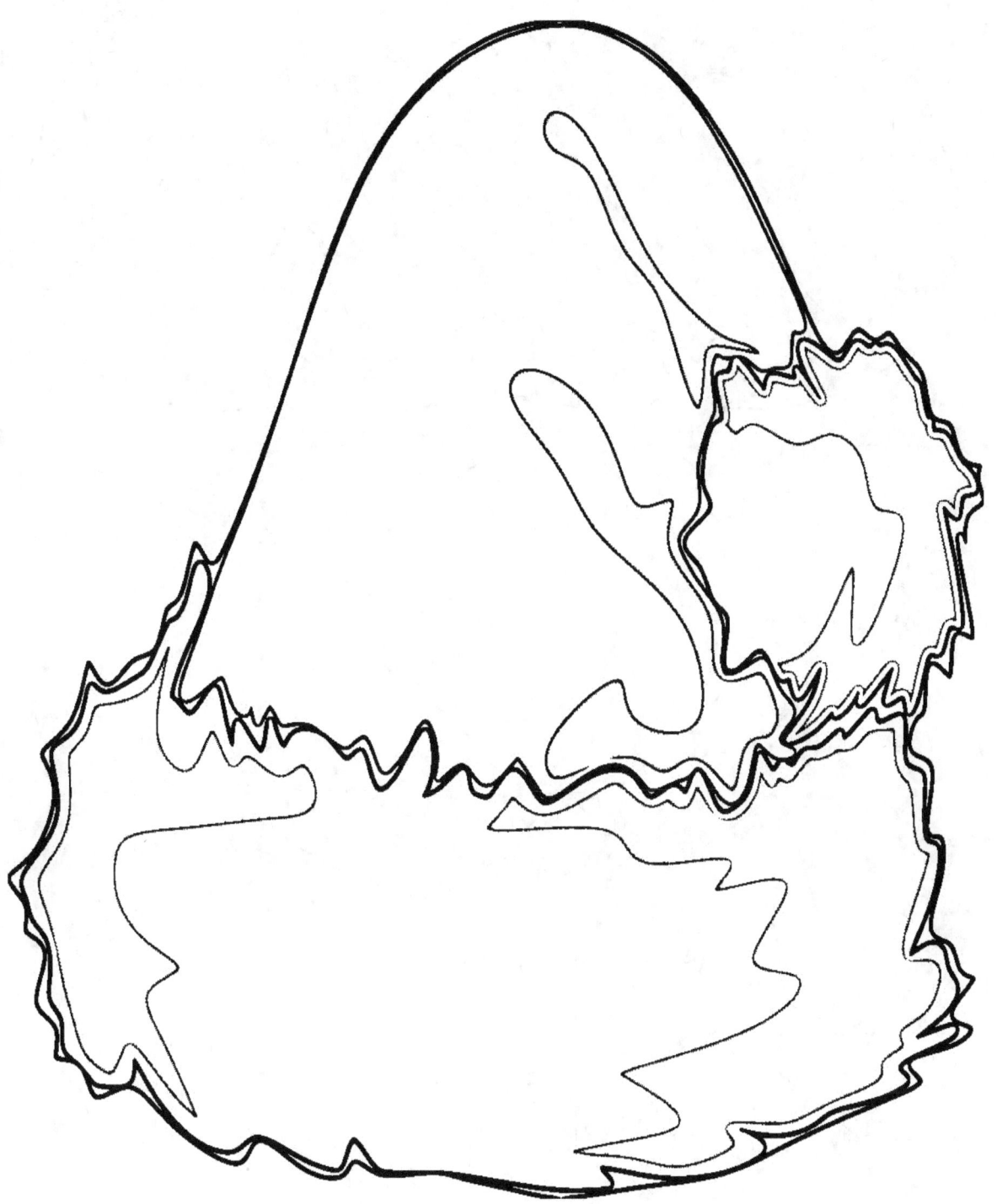

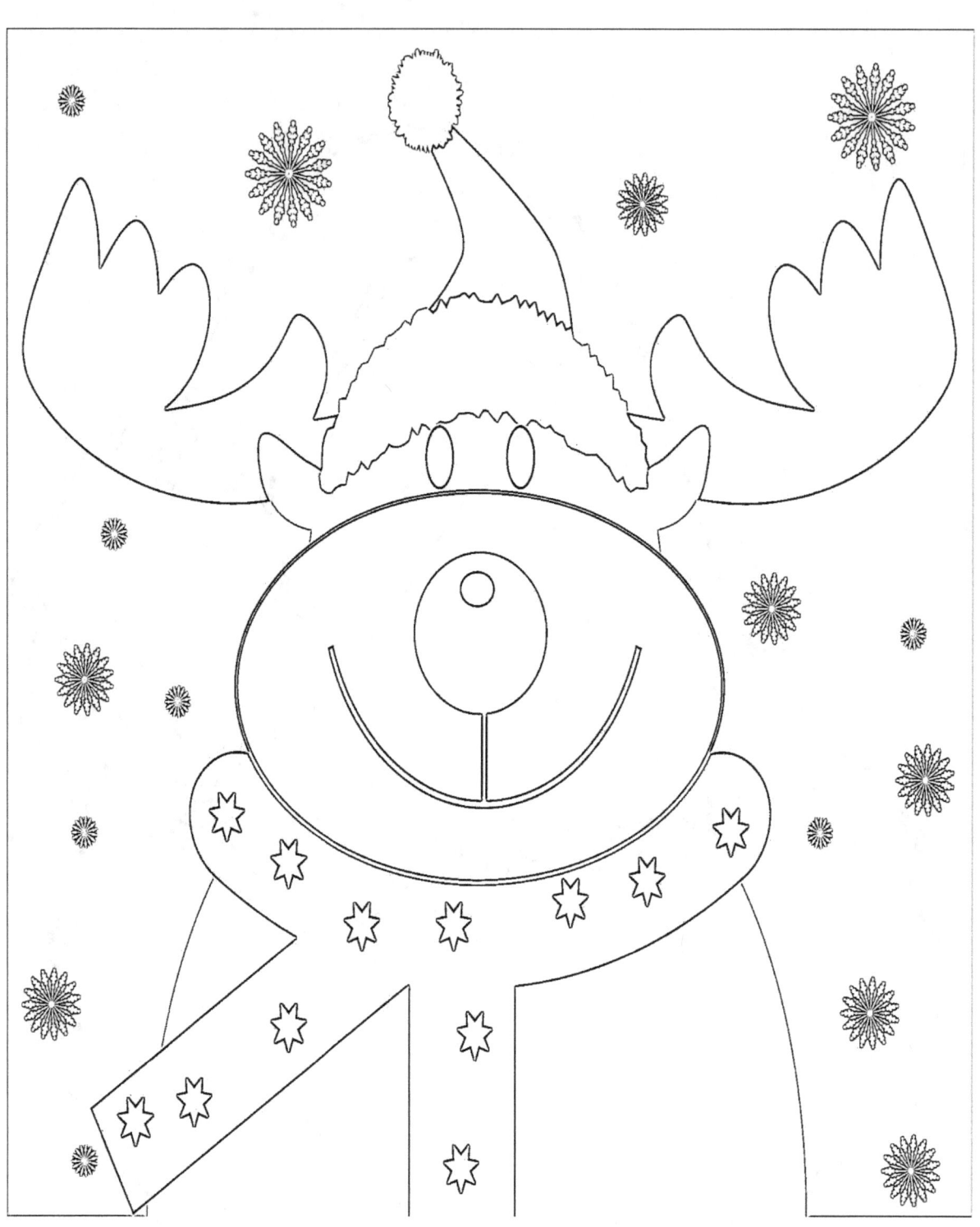

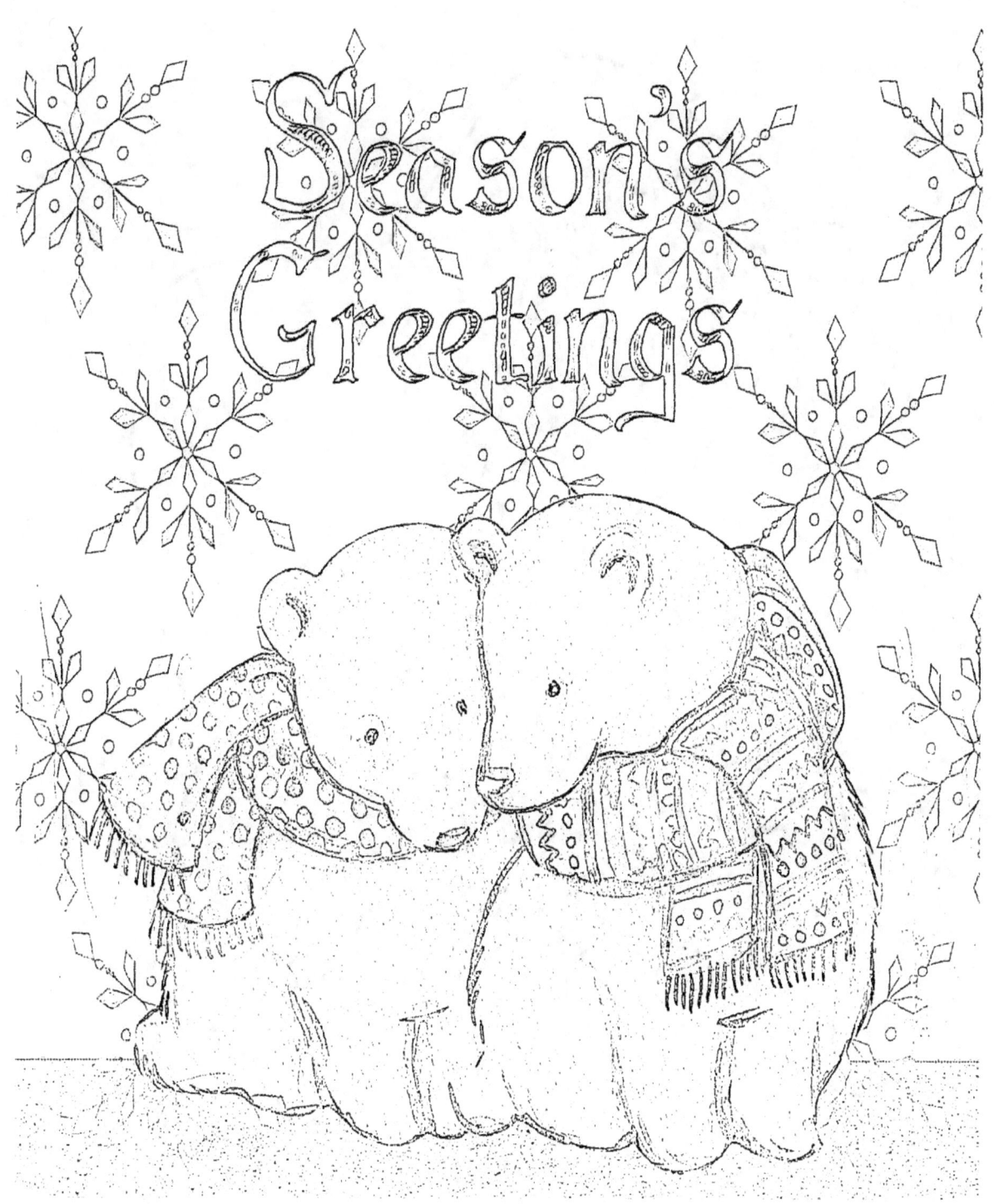

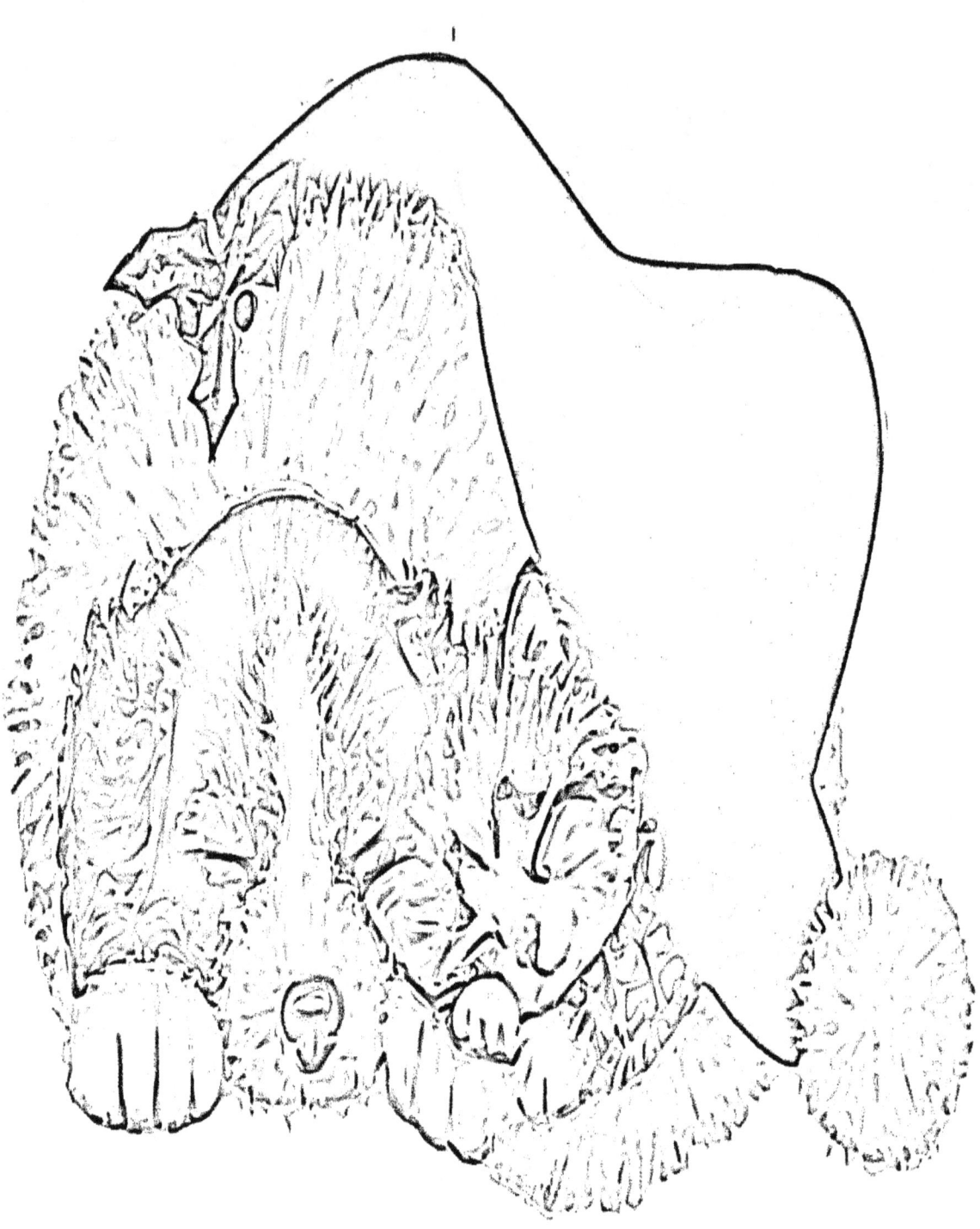

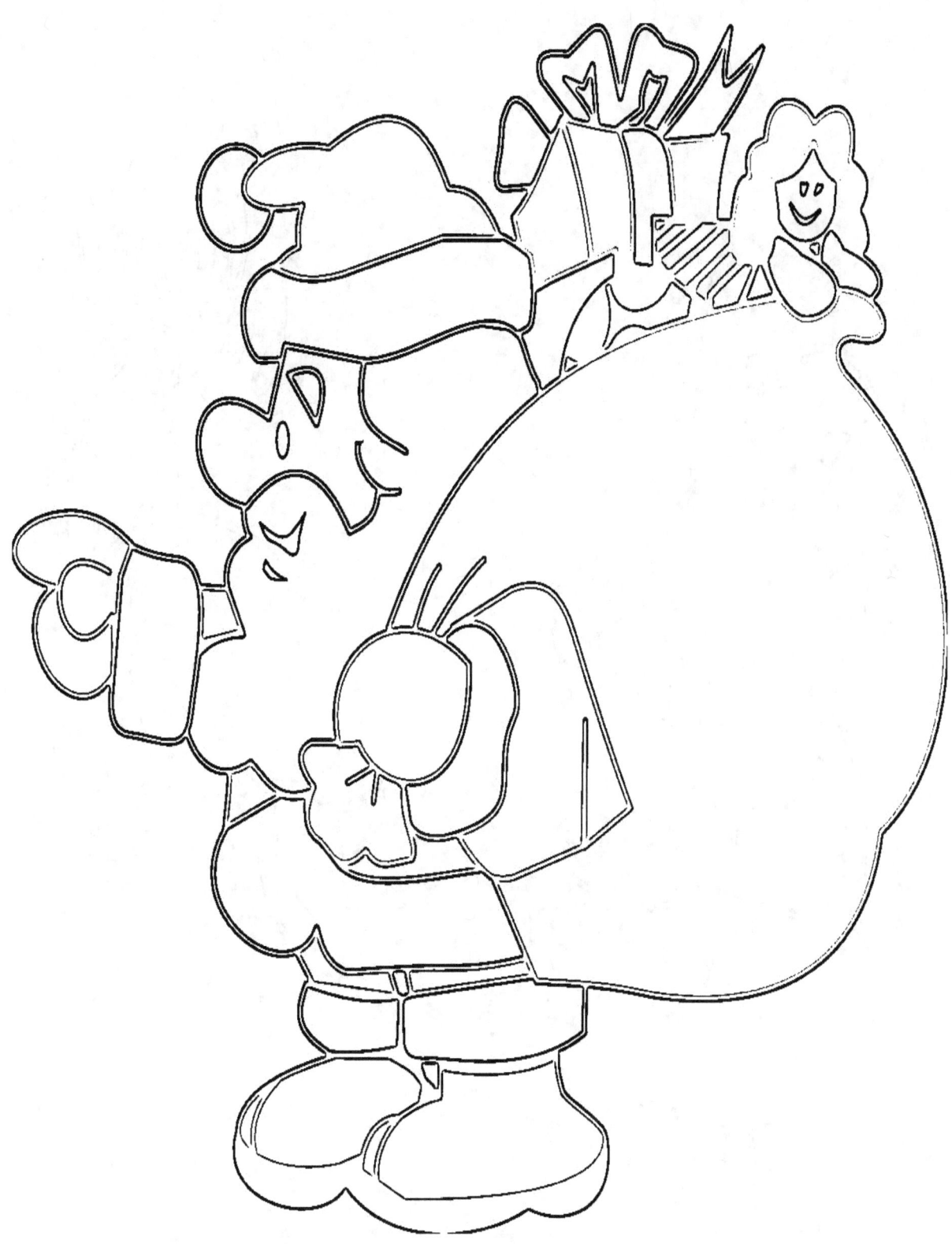

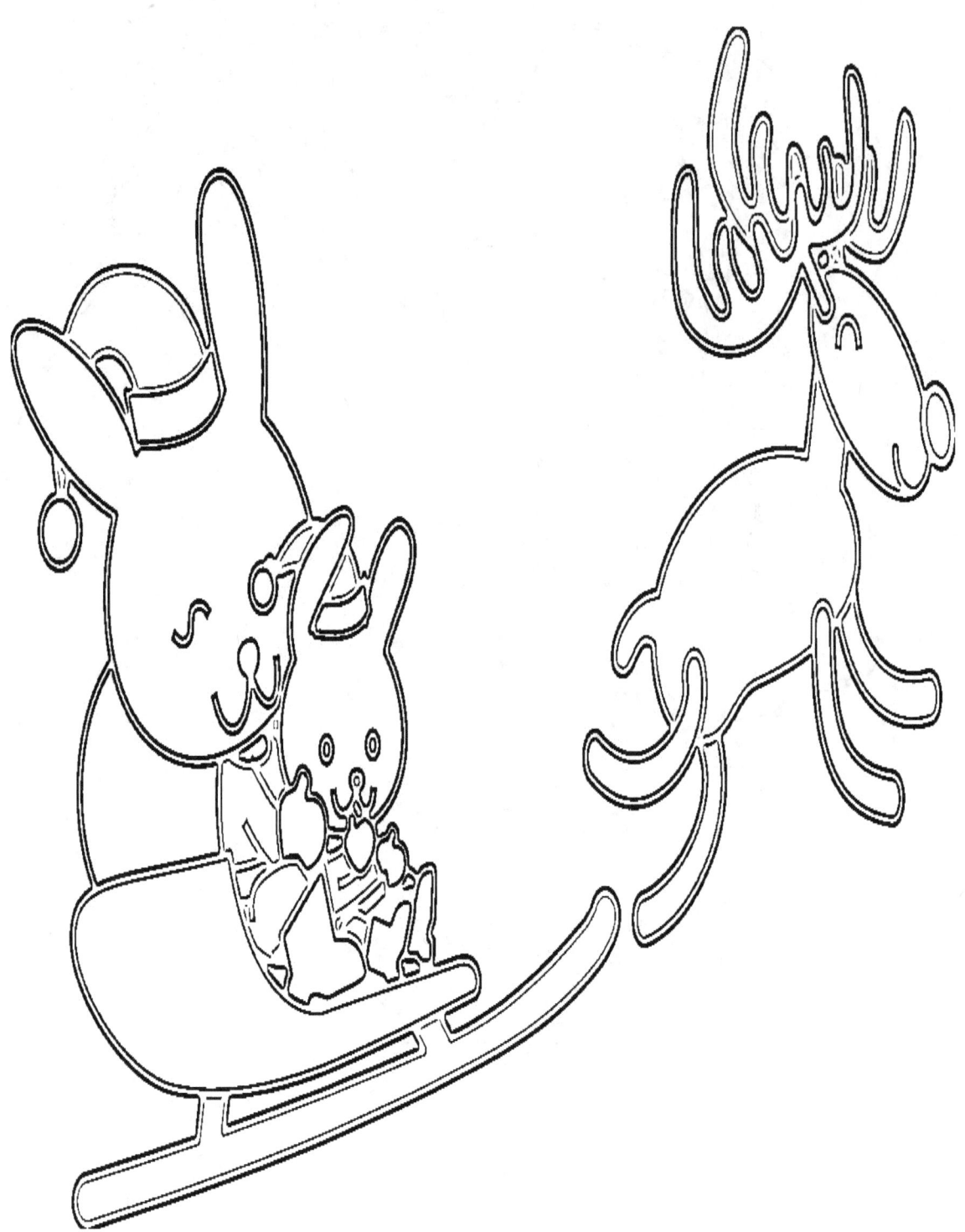

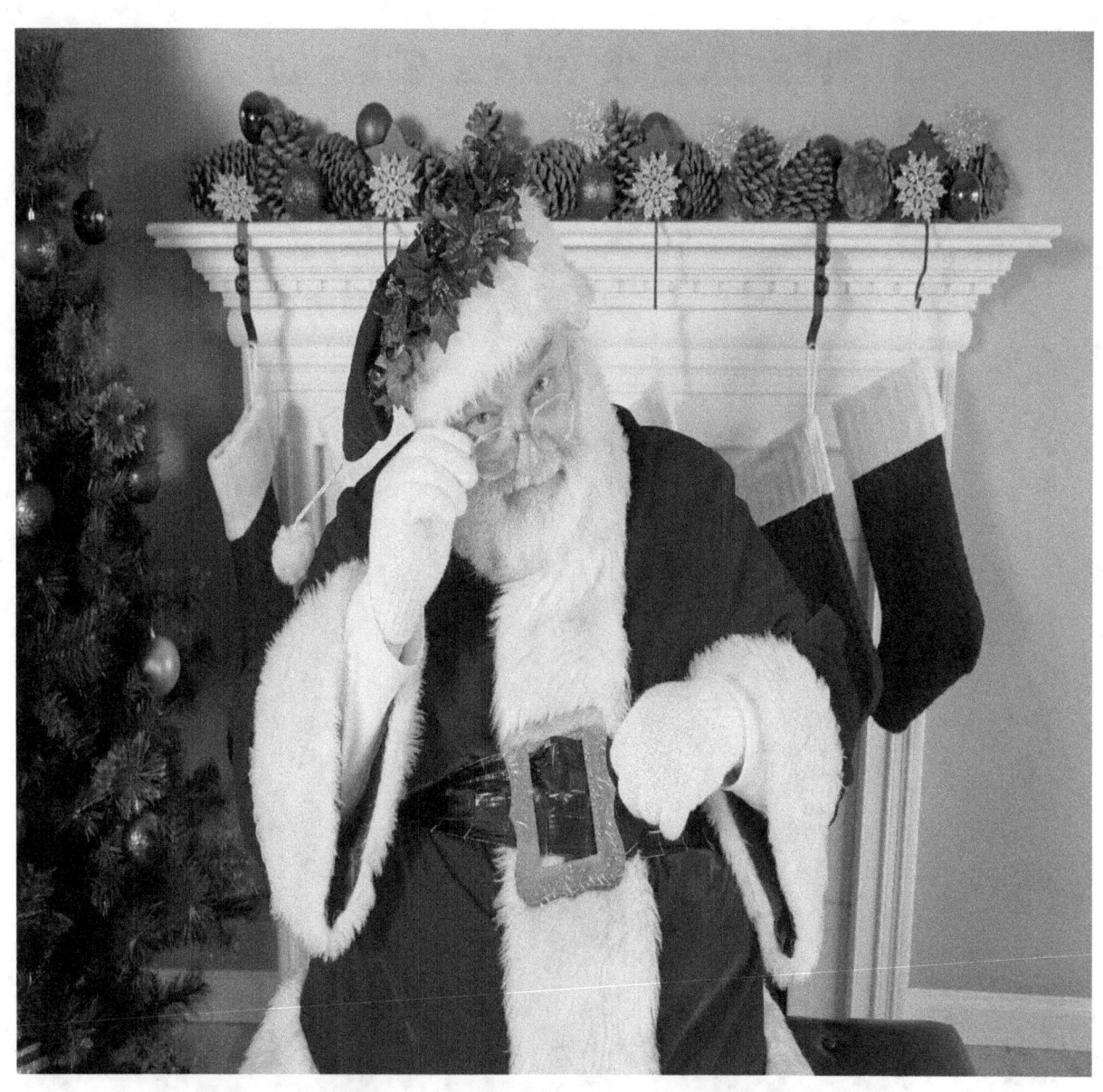

Ho, Ho, Ho......Merry Christmas

Love, Santa

Mr And Mrs Claus Making Their Appearance

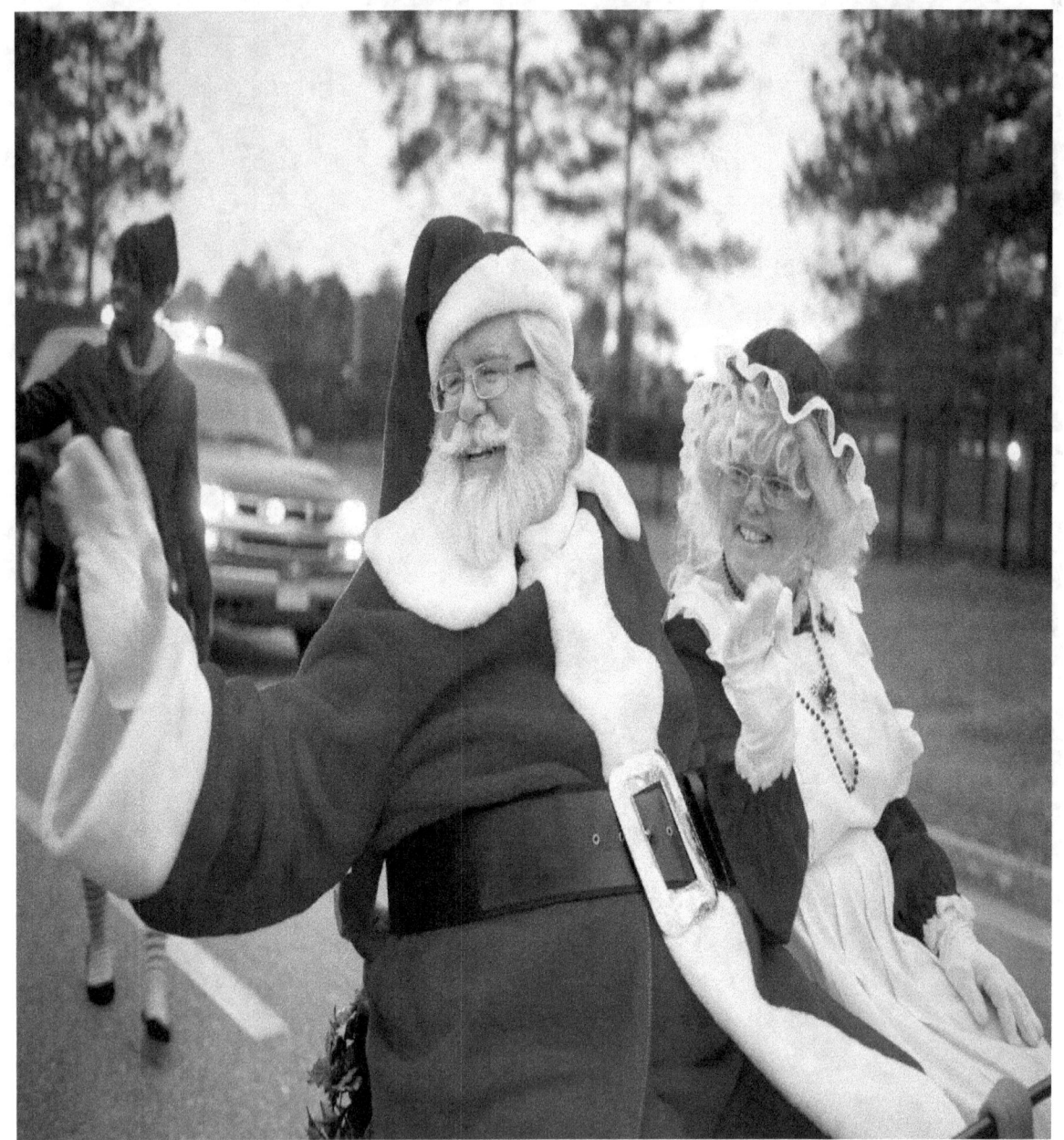

In A Christmas Parade

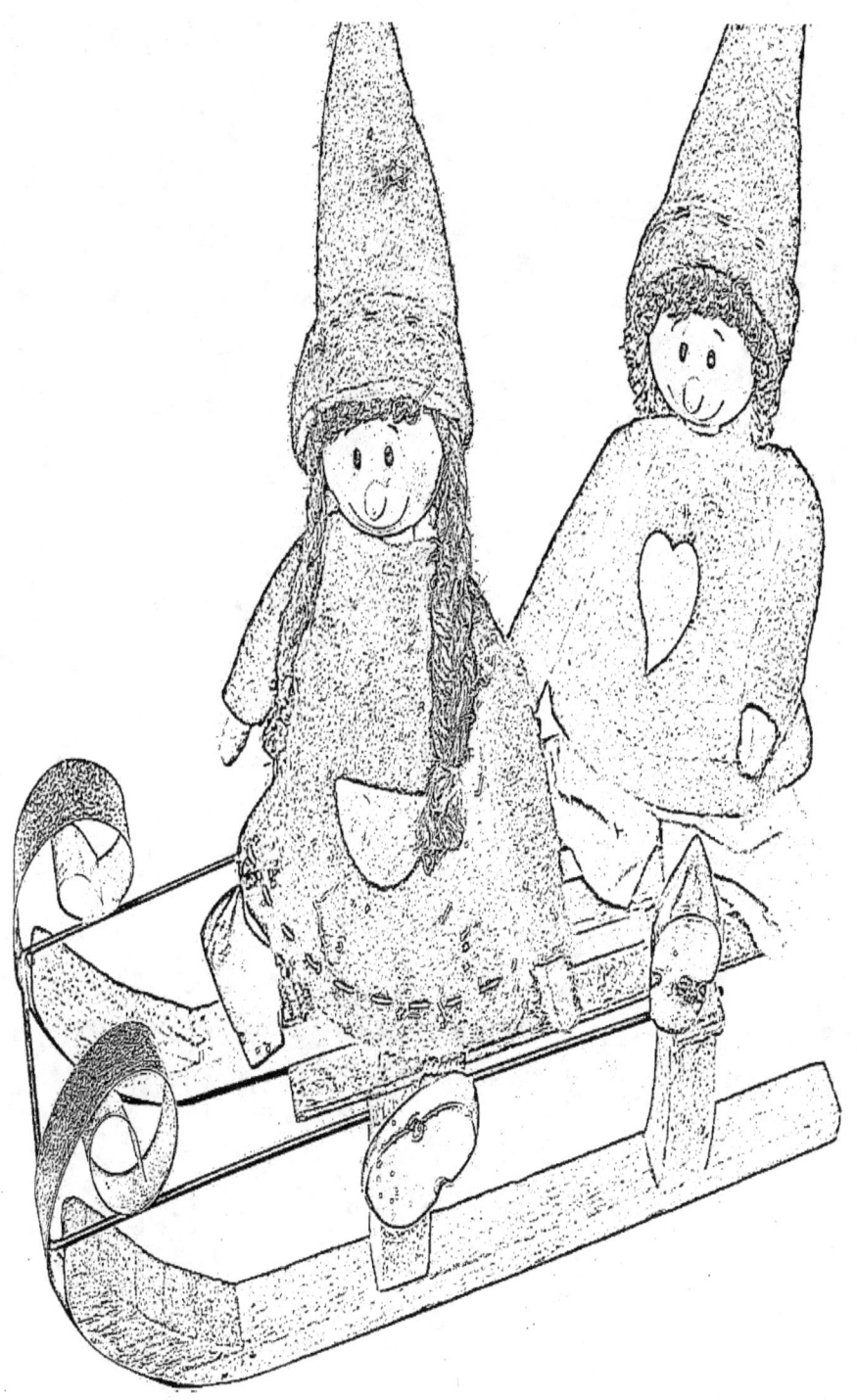

www.ingramcontent.com/pod-product-compliance
Lightning Source LLC
Chambersburg PA
CBHW062333220526
45469CB00008B/2702